PAINS IN THE OFFICE

FOR WAGE SLAVES EVERYWHERE

PAINS IN THE OFFICE

50 PEOPLE YOU ABSOLUTELY, DEFINITELY <u>MUST</u> AVOID AT WORK

ANDREW HOLMES AND DAN WILSON

CAPSTONE

First published 2004 by
Capstone Publishing Limited (a Wiley Company)
The Atrium, Southern Gate
Chichester, West Sussex, PO19 8SQ
www.wileyeurope.com
Email (for orders and customer service enquires): cs-books@wiley.co.uk

Reprinted October 2004

ISBN 1-84112-615-2

Designed and typeset by Baseline, Oxford, UK
Printed and bound in Great Britain by TJ International Ltd, Padstow, Cornwall
This book is printed on acid-free paper responsibly manufactured from sustainable forestry
in which at least two trees are planted for each one used for paper production.

Substantial discounts on bulk quantities of Capstone Books are available to corporations,
professional associations and other organizations.

For details telephone John Wiley & Sons on (+44) 1243-770441, fax (+44) 1243-770571 or email
corporatedevelopment@wiley.co.uk

Contents

Pains –
a catalyst for change

Who would have believed it? *Pains on Trains* was a great success, a bestseller and of course a great read. But wait a minute, there's more to this Pain-Spotting business than meets the eye. It has actually changed the way we commute. No sooner had the Broadsheet been exposed than the quality newspaper publishers started to ditch their broadsheet formats in favour of tabloids. First the *Independent*, then *The Times*. There's only three left – the *Guardian*, the *Financial Times* and the *Telegraph*, but I am sure it won't be long before they succumb to the power of Pains. Then a student at Chichester University, Hannah Watts, decided to base her dissertation on my book and staged a play in a mocked-up tube carriage. All your favourites were there, the Pervert, the Broadsheet, the Sleeper and the Traveller. I have also heard of avid Pain Spotters identifying and ticking off the Pains as they journey to and from work.

The phenomenon of Pains is changing the way we think and they way we behave. So it's time to turn our attention to the next environment which needs some drastic surgery – work. *Pains in the Office* will explore the dark side of the work environment and expose many of your colleagues who have been put on earth to upset, depress and annoy you. It's the perfect antidote to nightmarish co-workers everywhere!

AH

Acknowledgements

like any book, there are always people who provide invaluable input. I would like to highlight a small number of these observant ladies and gentlemen. James McColl, Martin Luther, Linda Latham, Elton Mayo, Andy Smith, Frederick Taylor, Nick Birks, Alistair Kett, Eric Cornish, Godert Van Der Poel, Sarah Tripp, Donna Peters and the host of people who would rather remain nameless. I would also like to thank Dan Wilson, the new illustrator who has made a fantastic job of injecting some additional and, at times, much needed humour; John Moseley, my editor at Capstone who helped to lighten the entries and of course Sally, who added her usual vital input. Boy, is she glad she doesn't have to work anymore.

The Joy of work

"My father taught me to work; he did not teach me to love it."
– Abraham Lincoln

I wonder just how many of us, given half a chance, would work. And by work I mean the standard scrape yourself out of bed on a Monday morning sort of work, not the vocational sort of stuff which really excites some, but by no means all. From the straw poll of the 2,872 workers I took whilst writing this book, it would be very few indeed. In fact, a paltry 14. The majority of us are economic refugees washed up on the shores of some unsuspecting company. Of course we all delude ourselves that the jobs we have are very interesting, immensely satisfying and are things that we had always wanted to do. In reality our current employers were probably the only people to offer us work. And we needed the cash… Such working lives fall way short of fulfilment, irrespective of what the management theorists might have us believe. This lack of fulfilment is reflected in the increasing trend within the working population to downshift in order to get a more satisfying life. One in four people over the age of 30 has voluntarily taken a job with lower pay because they want an easier life in exchange for a drop in income of around 40 per cent. Another survey of the over-forties found that 65 per cent felt they were in the wrong job. And, finally, a survey which investigated how happy people were at work found that, for the most part, very few of us were extremely happy in our jobs. And it seems the more swanky the job (accountants, architects, pharmacists and IT experts), the lower the happiness. The converse was true, with hairdressers being far happier. Interestingly only 4 per cent of estate agents were extremely happy in their work (they probably deserve it though, don't they, after all they don't make us particularly happy either). Such surveys suggest that many of us have had enough of the testosterone-fuelled workplace where we are treated worse than slaves. We would rather be digging up rotten potatoes and eating stale bread. Another fascinating trend is the high-powered executive giving it all up to become a teacher. Apparently these people want to give something back to society. If only the toerags on the receiving end were a bit more appreciative...

I occasionally muse on why all the fat cat and celebrity CEOs, who are extraordinarily wealthy, continue to work. Out of the entire working population, these are the lucky few; they have the opportunity to give it all up and pursue an amazing portfolio of other interests. But they don't. All I can imagine is that they are scared of growing old, losing the only source of self-worth they have and having nothing to look forward to but infirmity and incontinence pants. But the thing I find most odd are those lottery winners who proclaim that winning two million quid will make no difference to their life and that they will be turning up to work next Monday. Just who are they kidding? Having won that sort of money, no one will want to talk to them anyway, so they would be better off at home watching daytime TV and thinking how to occupy their incredibly small and unimaginative minds.

Of course, work is a necessity and one which the majority of us must endure for 30–40 years if only to keep the roofs over our heads, feed and clothe our families and put what little aside we can to survive old age. But why has the workplace become such a nightmare? And why do so many of our workmates drive us round the twist?

WAR, DARWINISM AND WORKSTROLOGY

I have three theories about work which shed some light on why there are so many Pains in the work setting. The first is the work is war theory, the second is the survival of the fittest (in essence, Darwinism) and the third is workstrology or star signs in the workplace. Of course, it is the third that people find the most interesting; everyone wants to believe that somehow their destiny is all mapped out by the stars and the fact that their boss is treating them like excrement is down to the fact that they are a Virgo and their boss a Taurus. Try telling that to a toilet attendant who has just slipped in some diarrhoea. Then, maybe, the diarrhoea is a Capricorn. Let's explore these three theories in a little more detail.

WORK IS WAR

There can be no doubt that the collective experience of the Second World War had a profound effect on everyone touched by it. Irrespective of whether those involved were frontline troops, the parents of those who lost their lives, or displaced and destitute civilians, the outcome was the same: a belief that the world deserved more humanity and that people should treat their fellow human beings with greater compassion and respect. The post-war world of work seemed to offer a wealth of opportunity that everyone was happy with. Employers were glad to get back (well, at least some) of the means of production and returning troops were glad to work in an environment where they didn't have to dodge bullets. Both employer and employee were conjoined in a happy and productive union. The work setting was benevolent, with the majority of people being treated with respect and having a reasonably good time of it. No long hours, no autocratic bosses, no backstabbing or infighting. This was the Harold Macmillan "you've never had it so good" era. For example, my father-in-law, who was an evacuee during the Blitz, spent his working life as a chemist with a major UK company. From the stories he has me told over the years, he had a fantastic time. There was a wonderful mix of focus, fun, excitement and camaraderie. The company would hold parties for staff, Christmas parties for their children and ship families to parts of Europe for social events. Contrasting this with the modern working environment highlights just how much has changed. Work has become more brutal, people have become more unfriendly and self-serving, and employers have become less bothered about treating staff with a modicum of respect. A significant minority have also become morally corrupt. There is a simple reason for this. As the collective experience of the horrors of the last war has attenuated, so has the way we treat our colleagues. Work is the new battlefield with the lead replaced by politics, the enemy by backstabbing and bullying workmates and the generals by oppressive, self-serving executives. It is just like war, with the Germans replaced by our colleagues – desperate for promotion, trying to deflect blame and generally looking out for numero uno.

SURVIVAL OF THE FITTEST

Darwin was right, we're all a bunch of animals (and this is nowhere more so than in the workplace). Evolution is a force that drives the male of the species and, increasingly, females, who seem to be becoming more masculine by the day. The basis of evolution lies in its ability to promote the fittest and weed out the weakest. The strong survive by passing on their genes to their progeny whilst the weak are generally left on the shelf to wither and die or are literally wiped out by the strong. We are driven by powerful forces that we find difficult to control; our primitive minds cannot be managed that well despite the emergence of the frontal lobes. Although society places controls over us so that we don't go round actually killing the weak and our enemies, don't be fooled into a false sense of security. They *are* out to get you, of that you can be certain. Therefore, we shouldn't be at all surprised at the some of the behavioural displays we see at work. Men (and women) will fight tooth and nail, using all their resources to become the top dog. They will eliminate anyone in their way. The strong and paranoid survive, destined to climb the greasy pole and protect their patch. The weak will fail to get promoted, may be asked to leave and will be the victims in the office. Those who aspire to great things will use a wealth of techniques to achieve what they desire: politics, blame, claiming to have done things they haven't and brown-nosing. The weak are just nice and get nowhere. It's a sad fact, but no one likes the nice guy. Well, not at work anyway. Recent research into equality suggests that those who fare worse in the world of work are likely to die sooner than those who do better. This is backed up by experiments with macaque monkeys. The researchers manipulated the social status of the monkeys whilst keeping other factors the same. High-status macaques from different troupes were put together to ensure some of them lost their status. The affected monkeys became ill and died prematurely. So there you have it, survival of the fittest is where it is at.

WORKSTROLOGY

There are those amongst the population who live under the false impression that the stars guide their destiny. They read their star signs every day in the belief this will somehow shed light on why their bosses are treating them like dirt or why someone has made an inhuman stench in the toilets. I'm sure they do this because it places the responsibility for their actions onto some celestial being rather than themselves. And what better place to do this than at work: "I'm sorry I haven't met that critical deadline, but my stars said I would be crap at work today." The whole basis of Workstrology lies in the fact that how we perform, how we are treated and how we relate to our colleagues lies in the stars. It is preordained and there is nothing we can do about it. So the next time you are called to account because of your non-compliance to the clean desk policy, it is highly likely that the person bawling you out is a Virgo. In a similar vein when you are getting a drubbing from some trumped-up little Hitler you can bet your bottom dollar that they are an Aries. Each star sign has certain characteristics and in order to both cope with them, and get the best out of them, you need to understand how the thousands of combinations of the fire, earth, air and water signs impact on the way work is executed. So chill out, the fact that your working life is so utterly futile has nothing to do with the inability of your current employer to use your latent capabilities, it's down to your mother and father and your ill-timed conception. Shit happens.

WORK WOULD BE GREAT... IF ONLY

So what do these theories mean? In simple terms they mean that you will spend the majority of your day dealing with a succession of Ball-Breakers, Bullies, Egotists, Butt Lickers, Control Freaks, Gossips and Competitors, to name but a few. We are thrown together in this false environment which we call work because of economic necessity and although we may come to like (or indeed love) some of our colleagues, there are plenty who will annoy us. They are our bosses, peers and subordinates. Each and every one of them has certain characteristics that we need to understand, become sensitive to and avoid at all costs. There is little point in discussing the relative merits of Taylorism (Scientific Management), Human Relations, Socio-Technical Theory or whatever our friends in Human Resources (HR) would like us to believe, because it makes not one jot of difference. Instead what I offer you is a new nomenclature, a new way of describing and discussing your work colleagues. This book will either transform the HR department or, ideally, eliminate it and it will change the way you are appraised and rewarded. So be warned, if you can see yourself in this book it might be time to change. So just as *Pains on Trains* has changed the nature of train travel, *Pains in the Office* will change how we approach work.

USING THIS BOOK

This book is all about those people who aggravate you at work. You may have already come across those people that annoy you on your journey into work (see Pains on Trains), and now it's time to witness how they make your life a misery in work. Taken together this means that for between 9–14 hours of your working day you are surrounded by people you would rather see swimming with concrete boots than working alongside you. The experienced Pain Spotters amongst you will know how to use this book, but for those who don't, it is designed in a way that allows you to spot your most hated colleagues, whilst at the same time expressing your own inner feelings in an accessible way. I am writing what you are thinking. Thus, in the same way that bird spotters identify the Lesser Spotted Warbler, this book helps you to spot the Corrupt Bastard, the Company Bike and the Bowel Mover. But it goes beyond that. It identifies how you can avoid them and seek your revenge – if you are brave enough. Each entry includes:

* The general characteristics of the Pain (including anecdotes and stories from fellow wage slaves).
* Their annoyance rating, which rates the Pain from 1 (limited annoyance) to 10 (extreme annoyance).
* Their rarity, which rates the Pain from 1 (exceptionally rare) to 10 (very common).
* Any seasonal variations, which will identify any seasonal changes to the Pain's behaviour.
* A range of avoidance/revenge strategies (with suitable escalation).

At the end of each entry I have also given you an opportunity to record that you have spotted the Pain and add your own annoyance rating. Like any "spotting" pastime, it has to be interactive, fun and have a sense of purpose. You might choose to swap entries with your friends and families and, god forbid, your fellow workmates (at least those you tolerate). This volume, when taken together with *Pains on Trains* and *Pains in Public*, provides you with 150 painful people who make your life less satisfying than it could be. Who needs self-help books, as when armed with the three Pains volumes, you can just avoid the jerks, muppets and morons who make life such a drag?

The Arse Coverer

GENERAL CHARACTERISTICS

There is a very simple theory for protecting your arse at work: the fan theory. The size of the fan you are permitted to have on your desk is proportional to your grade. So the higher up you are in the organisation, the bigger the fan. Whenever the shit hits the fan, everyone reaches out for the "on" button. The simple laws of physics then come into play, with the larger fans dispersing all of the shit, and the smaller ones scattering virtually none. So, you've guessed it, if you happen to be quite low down in the company you will be the one who ends up being covered in shit. Fans aside, in the world of work we increasingly have to protect ourselves against unscrupulous colleagues who will seek to blame us for anything that goes wrong, even if it wasn't our fault. Moreover, there are plenty of bosses who will ball us out if we so much as smile. For example, one poor chap, who worked as a fettler in an iron foundry, had to suffer regular drubbings from the charge-hand. Apparently he would stand behind this guy patiently waiting for him to cock something up and when he did, would shout at him (he had to, really, given all the noise). He would then move on to someone else, only to return a few minutes later to repeat the exercise. Eventually, the victim would leave a couple of perfect flanges hidden next to his workstation, so that when the charge-hand was on his way back he could whip out the pristine examples and pretend to work on them. Fortunately, the charge-hand was such a moron that he never quite worked out what was going on. It seems that fear rules all too many workplaces and keeping our heads down and avoiding the crossfire is now an occupation in its own right. So as the theatre of war has shifted from the battlefields of France to the battlefields of the office, the number of Arse Coverers has increased dramatically. The Arse Coverer is characterised by an unhealthy obsession with process,

paperwork and procedure. They are the bureaucrats who give bureaucracy a bad name. They will ensure that every base is covered before committing to anything, which inevitably slows down the pace of any task, especially the urgent ones. They are so well-versed in the specific rules, regulations and legalities of their work that when something does go awry there is no way they are going to carry the can. They are masters of record keeping so that, when the time comes, their backsides are well and truly titanium coated. They will come back with such statements as:

- "I'm so sorry, but you did not follow the correct procedure."
- "Yes, I know this is not perfect, but you really should have read the small print."
- "The job isn't finished until the paperwork is done." I fully suspect they say this to themselves when on the toilet.

Recently we heard of the untimely deaths of an elderly couple whose gas was cut off. The company who supplied the fuel blamed the fact that they had not informed Social Services of the poor couple's increased vulnerability on the Data Protection Act. Typical arse-covering behaviour. Arse Coverers love to hold positions allowing them to laud it over everyone else. So jobs like Quality Manager, Health and Safety Officer, Auditor, Risk Manager and Security Guard are perfect for them. In such roles they not only cover their own arses, but attempt to cover everyone else's too. There's a thought. One women informed me of her role as a quality guru. She helped to develop a monstrous quality management system for her IT department. During a six-month period she produced tons of procedures and instructions which were nothing short of impenetrable. Once complete, she had to police the whole thing, identifying defects and grassing people up for non-compliance. It wasn't long before everyone was up in arms and developing a whole variety of excuses to cover their arses. In the end, the whole thing was dropped because staff were spending more time covering themselves than actually working.

ANNOYANCE RATING

10 – Arse Coverers are annoying because they insist on doing everything by the book with no shortcuts: no cutting corners, nothing. They also do little by way of work. They give the appearance of being very busy, but if you asked them what they had actually delivered, they would probably stare at you with a blank face. Even they don't know.

RARITY

7 – Apparently no one wants to take risks these days. Everyone is so obsessed about slipping up and getting the sack that most people have arse-covering tendencies. I guess that in the world of the risk averse the Arse Coverer is king. A close ally of the Arse Coverer is the Jobsworth. When faced with a simple course of action that anyone with an ounce of common sense would follow, they will say with a sharp intake of breath: "That's more than my job's worth, mate!" The Jobsworth lives in a world of petty officialdom and loves every clause and sub-clause: "The Queen of Sheba may be visiting today, but parking her car in a space reserved for a director just ain't on; rules is rules!"

SEASONAL VARIATIONS

There are two seasonal variations that the Pain Spotter should be aware of. The first is the year-end Arse Coverer who will be typically involved in the **end of year** accounting processes. These fellows are expert at covering their tracks so that not even the most experienced auditor can spot them. The second is the project-based Arse Coverer, who appears near the **end of a failing project**. These are the people who will refer you to a long list of risks that you should have managed and, in essence, are blaming you for the failed project when they should be carrying the can.

AVOIDANCE/REVENGE STRATEGIES

1. Always work for people who are willing to take a risk or two and aren't fanatical about processes or paperwork.

2. Give the Arse Coverers some toilet roll so they can clean their arse, not just cover it.

3. Get hold of the rule book and smash them over the head with it.

4. Phone Crimewatch and report them for making everyone's life a misery. Include a mug shot for good measure.

5. Pose as Winston Churchill and say: "Never, in the field of human officialdom, have so many had so much value extracted by so few".

☐ Tick here when you have spotted the Arse Coverer

The Ball-Breaker

The received wisdom is that having women in the workplace is a wonderful thing. They bring a degree of calm and softness to the office, thereby reducing the levels of testosterone and competitiveness. This can make work a truly rewarding experience. This is true, so long as they are not obsessed with becoming men. Sure, there are many more women in the workplace these days and the glass ceiling is gradually being chipped away, but those women who insist on becoming more like men than the real thing are surely missing the point. The Ball-Breaker is someone who wants to emulate the male attributes of the office, including bullying, macho positioning and competitiveness. A recent survey showed that, among the under 35s, women outstrip men in their determination and commitment to succeed. Distorting Professor Higgins' question from *My Fair Lady* – why does a woman want to be more like a man? Is it that they want the increased weight, reduced life expectancy, thinner hair and shorter temper that men have? It seems they do. They'll be wanting female urinals next (for those interested, there was one attempt to market just these by the Urinette Company, who despite their best efforts to promote the She-Inal, failed abysmally). There are some interesting varieties of Ball-Breaker around, including:

- **The Testosterone Tarts**, who will use gels, patches, injections and implants to fuel their rooster-like behaviour. Apparently women MPs have been prescribed the hormone to help them compete in the debating chamber and there have been cases of high-achieving women taking testosterone supplements to enhance their work-based performance. If the dose is too high the user can end up with increased body hair, acne and a deeper voice. So the next time you notice a female colleague wearing a red suit, sporting a rather fancy moustache and booming in an excellent baritone, you might ask if she has overdosed on testosterone.

- **The Red-Suited Witches** who pride themselves on wearing the best tailored suits in the most vibrant of colours, often coupled with deep red lipstick, nail varnish and stiletto heels with which to crush the men beneath them. These women are fearsome men-haters.
- **The Superficial Supermums** who like to portray the image that they can do everything. This notion that there are such things as supermums out there is, of course, bunkum. Ball-Breakers who purport to hold down incredibly important and stressful jobs and yet still be capable of bringing up their three children single-handed are fake. The press loves to emphasise such superhuman abilities, but in reality such high-powered women employ a host of servants including live-in nannies, child minders, personal shoppers, cooks, cleaners, gardeners and probably the odd gigolo or two. And the rest. Let's face it, many of these Ball-Breakers probably didn't want children in the first place. It was their biological clock that forced them to have them (or so I have been told by a number of such women). So the next time you hear or read about some high-flying female executive who looks after her seventeen children under the age of five, works fifty hours a week for a local charity and runs a scout group, just spare a thought for her band of helpers.

I was told of one Ball-Breaker who was fearsome and would destroy anyone in her path. Men and women alike would quake before her and do all they could to keep her happy – which was, as you'd expect, difficult. Over the years, she discredited those around her so that she could reach a senior management position (typical of the Competitor). Then it went too far. She attempted to bully a member of staff into a role she wasn't prepared to do and when the poor lady refused to move, she got the sack. Things got out of hand with the union getting involved and before long the Ball-Breaker was on "long term sick". Eventually she resigned. Then there are the Ball-Breakers who abuse their power by offering sex to the younger male employees – why? Because they can. But what's good for the goose is good for the gander.

ANNOYANCE RATING

6 – It's a shame that Ball-Breakers have to be so masculine. But then, in a male dominated workplace, you can't blame them. In the end it is a sad reflection on both parties, not just the women. But why do they have to adopt all of the male traits which are considered so bad? Surely they are better than that. The last thing anyone wants to see is some highly strung woman behaving like a man. If we wanted that we'd have blokes dressing up in skirts all the time.

RARITY

7 – As the Y chromosome, and the men to whom it belongs, gradually fades away, the world of work will become dominated by Ball-Breakers, where women can run around like reincarnated Amazons, not needing men for anything. Well, maybe one thing – but with medical science speeding this evolutionary path along, it won't be long before men can be completely discarded. This is the ultimate fantasy of the Ball-Breaker who has little time for men and considers them weak, superfluous and idle. Perhaps a thousand years from now we can look forward to legislation that prevents discrimination against men who are paid less than women in the workplace, are slaves in the home and are generally treated as sex objects.

SEASONAL VARIATIONS

None. I don't believe there are many seasonal variations in the Ball-Breaker's behaviour. Once they are hooked on the testosterone-driven environment they cannot stop. You may find a monthly cycle, though, as the Ball-Breakers will gear themselves up for the regular board meetings in which they must dominate and prove yet again that they are worthy of their position of über bitch.

AVOIDANCE/REVENGE STRATEGIES

1. Ask the Ball-Breakers if they are suffering from adrenal hyperplasia.

2. Offer them an oestrogen patch to help reduce the excessive amounts of testosterone in their bloodstream.

3. Set up a self-help group called Testosterone Anonymous and invite them along to sit in a circle and talk about their testosterone addiction and how badly they were treated as children.

4. Leave articles lying around about famous Ball-Breakers who have thrown in the towel to spend more time with their families.

5. Do your best to make them cry so that they can, at last, show their feminine side.

☐ Tick here when you have spotted the Ball-Breaker

RATE THE **BALL BREAKER'S** ANNOYANCE

The Body Beautiful

∫ top press. Your looks will make a difference to your career. Like it or not, if you're ugly, short, obese, bald or just plain weird you may as well forget any notion of having a high-powered career and sweep the streets. Depressing though this might sound to the average ugly git, it is backed up by academic research. The penalty for being hideous is not insignificant, but what's surprising is that it is greater in men than women. Apparently a bloke who looks more like the Hunchback of Notre Dame than Brad Pitt earns around 10 per cent less than the standard-looking chap, whilst the more attractive ones amongst us earn 5 per cent more. The differential in women's income is less pronounced, with the Plain Janes bringing home 5 per cent less than average and the Miss Worlds 4 per cent more. Then, of course, there is baldness. The poor tappers amongst the working population suffer quite badly. Baldness sends out a message of decay. It is well known, for example, that those United States presidential candidates sporting a full head of hair tend to win elections. And what about make-up? Employers take women more seriously if they wear make-up. Those who don't are considered to be uninterested in their careers and not team players, and it is female bosses who believe this more strongly. What's more, those who do wear it earn 30 per cent more than those who don't. So unless you look the part, you won't cut it, no matter how clever you are or how much you suck up to the boss.

With this in mind, it should come as no surprise at all that there will be people in your office who are obsessed about their image and looks. They are the Body Beautifuls. Body Beautifuls will do everything in their power to look good and feel good. From the well-manicured hands (grubby hands send out all the wrong signals... unless you're a bored

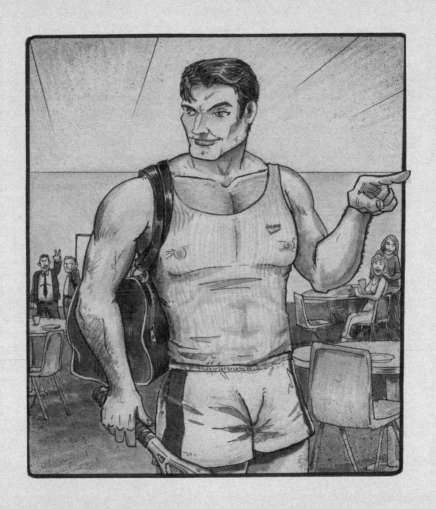

housewife, in which case a bit of rough might be appealing), to the excessive use of beauty products, they are focused exclusively on how they look. They want that edge that sets them aside from the drab competition. They will go on and on about their tailored clothes and the gym they go to (which they will attend almost every lunchtime or after work. I overheard one guy giving another chap a lecture on how he likes to go down to his gym at least twice a week and augments it with hundred-mile bike rides every weekend… who cares, exactly?). The Body Beautiful will follow and, of course, adopt the latest diet and exercise fads in order to maintain their ideal figure. They are fans of botox, removal of excess hair, which for men is known as BCS (back, crack and sack), Atkins (see also the Diet Bore) and in fact anything so long as it enhances their looks. So for all you Body Beautifuls out there, why not try beer? It appears that drinking a pint of bitter is capable of keeping your skin looking youthful. The silicon it contains is easily absorbed into the bloodstream which in turn maintains the amorphous material between the protein-based collagen and elastin fibres that makes skin bouncy and stretchy. Mind you, if you drink a few dozen pints a week you might have lovely looking skin, but your liver will be shot to bits; the Body Beautiful meets the Boozer. The Body Beautiful can, of course, go a little too far in the pursuit of perfection. They often turn to anabolic steroids which promote cell growth and repair. In fact the Body Beautiful typically takes more than fifty times the recommended dose of such substances. The problem here of course is that they interfere with other parts of the body; in particular, the genitals. For men this means that as muscle tone improves the size of the penis diminishes to the point where you can't distinguish it from a pine needle. So, girls, the next time you are propositioned by some smooth, suave and well-built male, just ask if they are suffering from "bigorexia". They may also have breasts, as these alien chemicals are transformed into oestrogen. Perhaps they are aiming to be the ideal employee, mixing male and female, and through this creating an office full of hermaphrodites.

ANNOYANCE RATING

2 – I suppose in the current obesity epidemic, in which we now live, and the rebound from the dress-down dot-com days, we ought to cut the Body Beautiful some slack. Let's face it, we would rather spend our working days with someone who looks well dressed and slim, than someone who is rotundly challenged, covered in grease and whose clothes smell and look as though they have never been washed or ironed.

RARITY

6 – The Body Beautiful is fairly common and is more so in companies located within major conurbations or cities which sport gyms and massage parlours. I think people who go to massage parlours normally expect some additional personal services and only wish to exercise certain parts of their anatomy, which may help to explain the glow they have on their return.

SEASONAL VARIATIONS

The Body Beautiful will be particularly visible during the **early months of the New Year**, as they will be very concerned that they have let themselves go over Christmas. Like the Diet Bore, they will be full on during the **summer months**, when they need to look their best for their overseas holidays.

AVOIDANCE|REVENGE STRATEGIES

1. Come to work in designer trainers and tell everyone that you ran in from home, which is 20 miles away.

2. Build a muscle beach in one corner of the office and invite the Body Beautifuls to smear olive oil over their bodies and pose.

3. Buy a rear-view mirror and attach it to the Body Beautiful's PC. They can then spend their day checking their hair, make-up, tie, and could even use it to squeeze the odd spot or two.

4. Conduct a survey into steroid abuse in the office.

5. Send out an email from the chief executive stating that under no circumstances should anyone go to the gym at lunchtime and that instead everyone should be eating burgers and chips.

☐ Tick here when you have spotted the Body Beautiful

*RATE THE **BODY BEAUTIFUL'S** ANNOYANCE*

The Boozer

There is nothing so satisfying as slumping into an armchair after a long day at the office and sipping a glass of your favourite claret. Having a couple after work is great way to unwind. But it seems that we are all taking this a little too far. We are now a nation of binge drinkers, which according to the latest research is costing businesses in the UK something in the region of £7 billion a year. Apparently up to 40 per cent of male and 20 per cent of female drinking sessions now qualify as binge drinking. And the percentage of women drinkers getting totally smashed is increasing more than that of men. The Boozer is someone whose only hobby is getting pissed and urinating their salary away. They will regale you with amusing stories of how drunk they were, how ill they were (as a result of getting terribly drunk) and of the various antics they got up to. Ever since the times of Henry Ford, drinking at – and indeed away from – work has been frowned upon. Ford even hired spies to check up on his workers and if any of them were found to have been drinking of an evening, they were sacked. Bosses have become a bit more relaxed these days, as coming into the office wrecked after a long boozy lunch is perfectly acceptable: especially if you happen to be the boss. I have heard of many instances of office staff rolling in blind drunk. I was told of one chap whose boozing started off quite innocuously on Friday lunchtimes. He would settle down in the pub at twelve o'clock and drift back to his desk a little after two. During this time his friends would watch in fascination as he sunk six pints in one session. No wonder he couldn't function when he returned. Soon he started boozing every lunchtime (he hated his job and had just finished a long-term relationship) and was often sent home because he was plastered. Boozers are easily spotted around the office with their telltale behaviours, which include:

- Breathing fumes over everyone – it's always easy to smell a Boozer when you haven't been drinking.
- Slurring their words.
- Becoming over-familiar with you, saying things like "I really luv you, I do," or touching your breasts (if you are a woman... let's not even go there if you are a man).
- Staggering, falling over and knocking into furniture.
- Falling asleep on the desk.
- Vomiting into waste bins.

I heard of another Boozer who was once found walking naked around a fashionable part of London after locking himself out of his house. He had gone to bed the night before tanked up. Then, in the early hours of the morning, he had gone out into the street whilst sleepwalking. Only when the heavy security door slammed shut behind him did he wake up. It was a bit embarrassing saying good morning to an old lady walking her dog, but he did so with some panache. A more extreme version of the Boozer is the Druggie, who will snort the odd couple of lines of white powder to get them through the day. This is apparently quite common in stressful jobs, where maintaining the edge is critical to success. I have been told stories by cabbies who have had many a City Boy taking coke in the back of their cabs. So the next time you see someone around the office who is full of the joys of spring, they might just be suffering from the excited delirium which often accompanies cocaine use. At least they won't smell like a brewery.

ANNOYANCE RATING

7 – A little bit of something you fancy is not a bad way to relieve the tedium of a monotonous existence. A swift one at lunchtime dulls the nerves and chills you out. The problem is that Boozers are a bit like Chimneystacks. They will put in fewer hours, stink and be less productive than their more sober colleagues. They also have this awful tendency to fall asleep, especially the older ones. They will throw many more sickies than the more sober amongst us. The introduction of Duvet Days, when an employee can ring in sick because of their antics of the night before, is testament to the level of drinking that goes on. Maybe employers should introduce a Pain Day, when you can have a day off to get some respite from all the pains you have to work with, including the Boozer.

RARITY

7 – The fact that so many people turn to the bottle is a clear indictment of the horrors of work. Most of us are crap at expressing our feelings, so what better way to release our frustrations than to down a few pints, glasses of wine or bottles of meths? As our working hours increase and we have to endure more time with people we would rather shoot, the number of Boozers is bound to grow.

SEASONAL VARIATIONS

As expected, **Christmas** and, indeed, **any office celebration** will bring out the Boozer in force. Here, of course, they have permission to go totally over the top and get completely bladdered. This will bring out some of the worst behaviours, including fist fights, women showing their knickers, plenty of vomit, mooning and all kinds of sexual antics (see the Lovebirds). It's also when the underling will go and tell the boss exactly what they think of him or her. Although this might have been a good idea at the time, the following day it seems somewhat crazy. But, hey, booze does loosen the tongue and softens the genitals.

AVOIDANCE/REVENGE STRATEGIES

1. Never drink during office hours.

2. Draw a straight line on the office floor and ask everyone who has been out drinking to walk along it. Those who fail to remain on the line are too drunk to work.

3. Book the Boozer into a rehab clinic along with the rest of the old soaks.

4. Walk around the office with a lighted candle and see if you can set fire to the Boozers' breath as they return from the pub.

5. Give them a lecture on the effects of alcohol on the liver and, better still, bring a pickled one into work to provide some added colour.

☐ Tick here when you have spotted the Boozer

RATE THE **BOOZER'S** ANNOYANCE

The Bowel Mover

GENERAL CHARACTERISTICS

If you're anything like me, the last place you want to evacuate your waste matter is at the office. I am sure the following is all too familiar to you. You're desperate and you wish you had been before you left the house that morning. You look towards the toilet to see if anyone is going in, in the hope that it will be empty. If there is someone in, you will find another facility well away from anyone you know. Once you have settled into your cubicle and are busily occupied you hear the door open. Oh no, what do you do? You don't want to be seen or heard. You sit there waiting for the other person to finish, or "complete the paperwork", in double quick time to ensure you get out before they do. Sheer trauma. Some say that retirement is a great leveller; I think doing a poo is. Let's face it, the boss has to go, so do the Bully, Egotist and Ball-Breaker. Now that's an image worth remembering when they are giving you a hard time.

The types of problem you face with the Bowel Mover include:

- **The noise.** Sitting there listening to someone fart uncontrollably and never seeming to drop anything significant is bad enough, but when this is followed by a pebble-dashing noise as the object of the hapless Bowel Mover's efforts are splattered around the bowl, it's just too much (for those interested this is a common condition known as diverticulitis. Diverticulae are small protrusions on the inner wall of the colon, which is where your residue is stored ready for elimination, and are very common in industrialised countries because of the lack of bulk in our diet. Apparently this allows muscle contractions to create localised areas of high pressure thus allowing the

diverticulae to form). Then there are the depth-chargers who summon up the largest stool in history in an attempt to smash the toilet. Unfortunately those responsible for such faecal material have a tendency to block up the u-bend, thereby preventing anything else from passing through to the sewers.

- **The stench.** Some people's insides must be rotten to the core as the smell would offend the devil himself. What's worse is when you are going into the toilet as they walk out; the smell that follows them is inhuman. And sometimes the Bowel Movers themselves don't have to be physically present: one poor chap worked in a gentleman's outfitter in a provincial market town which had a problem with the drains. All too frequently they would fracture and the basement, where he had the misfortune to work, would be filled with the most unearthly smells you could imagine. It was as though the bowels of the entire population of the town had been emptied into the room.

- **The mess.** Clearly some Bowel Movers would be more at home in the farmyard than the office. Such people leave skid marks in the bowl, toilet paper all round the floor (some of which still has excrement on it), floaters, or just everything.

The good news is that people are willing to take direct action to capture and embarrass the offenders. In one organisation a group of men devised a trap to catch the Bowel Mover. This consisted of a large grizzly bear (unfortunately, only a stuffed one) on a wire that would fall down and trap the stinker when the lavatory was flushed. One group of women who worked in an advertising agency would leave messages to the Poo Queen, a woman with limited water closet skills, requesting her to clean up the mess she so often left in the loos. My wife, on hearing and smelling the Bowel Mover in action, would rush out to her colleagues to get them to all stare and laugh when the woman came out: and it was usually her supervisor. And we should not forget the toilet police in Singapore who will chase you down the street if you fail to flush the bog after dropping your guts. I was recently informed of a Proud Stinker, who would spend about twenty minutes in the toilet only to return to announce to his colleagues that "I wouldn't go into the gents for a while." Not long after the announcement, there would be a queue outside the disabled toilet while staff waited for the stench to clear in the other one.

ANNOYANCE RATING

7 – Although the Bowel Mover can't help having to go, for which we ought to cut them some slack, it's the god awful stink they make, the terrible noise of their flatulence and evacuated material hitting the pan that is so annoying. Why don't they soften the blow by placing a layer of tissue on the water before setting to with the task in hand? The real problem lies in the fact that many of us are mysophobics who have a pathological fear of being exposed to the insanitary or disease-producing substances of which the Bowel Mover is king.

RARITY

10 – The call of nature is far too strong and anyone who says that they don't have a dump at work is either a liar or has had their sphincter sewn up.

SEASONAL VARIATIONS

None, but I can't say I have ever spent long enough in a toilet to discover seasonal variations in the Bowel Mover's toiletry habits. However, I am sure there are people out there who have, as in these cosmopolitan days there will be the odd stool fetishist about. I think there are likely to be more variations connected to food consumption. I'm sure that a proctologist would have plenty to say about diet. The old adage that you poo what you

eat comes to mind. And, of course, we should always remember what happened to Elvis – exploding on the loo isn't the best way to go, which gives a whole new meaning to "dying on the job".

AVOIDANCE|REVENGE STRATEGIES

1. Learn to control your bottom muscles so that you never have go to the toilet in the office.

2. Photograph the Bowel Mover as they come out of the toilet. Tell them that you have been appointed as the new office bottom inspector and you're collecting the details of the worst offenders.

3. Place clingfilm across the bowl (but below the seat). Let's see them clear the mess up after that.

4. Install a closed-circuit television or similar device in the cubicle together with a microphone and relay the Bowel Mover's antics to a wide-screen television in the office.

5. Just before the Bowel Mover enters the closet, pour hydrogen peroxide all over the pipes behind the toilet. This will corrode the pipes and before long they'll have one almighty mess on their hands... literally.

☐ Tick here when you have spotted the Bowel Mover

RATE THE
BOWEL MOVER'S
ANNOYANCE

The Bully

The Bully is one of the most evil pains you will see at work. Bullies are responsible for millions of sick days every year, low productivity and a general lack of trust in the workplace – and they are on the rise. Indeed, bullying is a global phenomenon. Their key to success is that they treat their staff like dog shite. They believe that coercion is the only way to manage subordinates and that anyone who shows humanity is weak. But before you ladies out there suggest that this is a male-only pain, I would like to highlight some interesting statistics. Some 58 per cent of bullies are women, and given that most victims are female this suggests that they are busy bullying their sisters more than the men around them. In fact, female bullies choose their own sex to bully 87 per cent of the time. Whatever their gender, Bullies are deeply insecure, with poor and usually non-existent social skills and as much empathy as a corpse. They have probably spent most of their childhood being beaten up by their parents, brothers, sisters, schoolchildren, gerbils and the occasional hamster. The result is someone who is incredibly driven to beat up other people, principally to make up for their immense insecurities and the fact that every one thinks they are an arsehole. Most Bullies come from broken homes and very poor backgrounds. I know of many who came from the back streets of inner cities or slums where they were mugged for their shoelaces. Interestingly, this type of background produces more CEOs than any other, as a poor, lower working class upbringing is one of the predicators to success. Such traumatic backgrounds remain with Bullies for the rest of their lives and, rather than seek professional help, they believe it's fine to treat those around them like excrement. The Bully comes in a variety of forms, including:

- **The Verbal Abusers** who will shout and scream at you in the same way children do when they can't get their way.
- **The Psychological Thugs** who will undermine their staff with subtle threats and attacks.
- **The Humiliators** who will come into a crowded room, shout and generally put down a member of staff.

Stories about the Bully abound and there is, thank heavens, plenty of opportunity for payback. One poor man worked for a Bully who would adopt the tactics of the Humiliator. He would choose his victim and then tower over them spouting a continuous stream of verbal abuse and vitriol until the victim would break down. Once this had been achieved, he would retire to his office having satisfied his lust and probably feeling quite good about himself. In time his staff made his life a misery by phoning him at three o'clock in the morning until he went ex-directory, ordering consignments of manure on his behalf and having them dumped on his drive and sending him hate mail in the post. He eventually retired to a life of deserved loneliness.

ANNOYANCE RATING

10 – Quite rightly, the Bully rates 10 out of 10 for annoyance. Their behaviour is unforgivable and it is encouraging that some organisations have been bold enough to do something about it. But beware: most Bullies hunt in packs. Cast your memory back to the playground when the Bully had to be surrounded by his or her cronies. The office is similar. Rarely do they work alone because if they did they would probably get a damn good kicking and end up crying like a big baby, which – of course – is what they are.

RARITY

9 – Unfortunately the Bully is far from rare and if anything is on the increase. My theory of work is war runs deep through the Bully. These are people who want to attack and destroy all before them. There is no humane side to them at all and in many respects they can be viewed as the latter-day guards of the death camps. They see their job as to break the inmates, destroy their resolve and undermine their spirit. They are also the modern day Hitlers and Stalins who can't cope with anyone who is better (or taller, see the Little Big Man) than them, or who exposes their incredibly low levels of self esteem. What is very worrying is the significant percentage of Bullies in public service. Apparently 20 per cent of Bullies are teachers, lecturers and school administrators, 12 per cent are healthcare

professionals, 10 per cent work in social services and 6 per cent in the voluntary sector. Now, that is ironic.

SEASONAL VARIATIONS

You may find more Bullies during the **winter months** when such things as seasonal adjustment disorder (SAD) reduce their already low levels of self-esteem.

AVOIDANCE/REVENGE STRATEGIES

1. Attach a picture of the Bully's face to a dartboard and see how often you can hit the eyes.

2. Ask them if they have any children. If they say "yes", tell them that they must hate them; if they say "no", respond "thank god". At least they won't be bringing more dictators into the world.

3. Send them a note that says "Those who can, do. Those who can't, bully".

4. Take out a contract on them. Apparently hiring a contract killer only costs £1,000; well worth the price. The increased productivity alone will more than cover the cost.

5. Scoop up a fresh dog turd, place it in an envelope and send it to their home address.

☐ Tick here when you have spotted the Bully

RATE THE
BULLY'S
ANNOYANCE

The Butt Licker

There are many things that attract us to other people in the office. Sex is an obvious one; personality is another, but power is perhaps the ultimate attractor. However, no matter how strong the attractions might be they tend to be short-lived, especially those associated with sex and power. So how can we explain the actions of the Butt Licker? The Butt Licker is the first of the sycophantic pains on the payroll. But, whereas the Competitor and Career Bike will only suck up to people who can influence their career, the Butt Licker is someone who will blow hot air up anyone who has any semblance of importance in the firm. These are truly sad individuals who will take every opportunity to compliment those in authority. Typical butt-licking behaviours include:

- Complimenting superiors on their dress sense, even when they look more like tramps than chief executives.
- Hovering around the bosses at social events like some kind of bad smell and taking every opportunity to quiz them on the latest business deal and the general economic environment.
- Asking the bosses about their home life. You know, how their kids and partner are, where they will be sailing their yacht this year and whether or not the tortoise, Ermintrude, is out of hibernation.
- Following the manager around the office like a lapdog, seeking out any job, no matter how menial, so that they can demonstrate their commitment and devotion.
- Believing in and practising the three Ks – who to kiss, what to kiss and when to kiss.

I heard of one Butt Licker who would employ most of the tactics above. The boss he attached himself to treated everyone exceptionally badly, bawling them out, dressing them down and generally making everyone's lives a misery. And yet our butt-licking friend could not see a bad bone in him. He would always say how clever he was and what a fantastic, caring boss he was, flying in the face of general opinion and defending the evil man. Everyone around the Butt Licker could not understand why this chap was so in love with the boss and thought there must be something odd about him. In the end, his sugary behaviour got too much to stand. So whilst the Butt Licker was out to lunch one Friday, a couple of his colleagues wrote an email to his boss on behalf of the Butt Licker expressing his innermost thoughts. But rather than telling the boss that he was really crap and awful to work with, thereby revealing that the Butt Licker had been lying all along, they decided to tell him that he was in love with him and that he wanted him to leave his wife and cohabit. The sincerity of the email was so convincing that the boss thought it was genuine and that he had better confront the Butt Licker before things got out of hand. He called the chap in. Naturally the Butt Licker was surprised and somewhat confused and had a hard time worming his way out of the predicament he found himself in. Nothing further was said and the Butt Licker's behaviour became suitably subdued. Perhaps Butt Lickers are not as stupid as they appear, as being brown-nosing nightmares may well ensure they are safe from the axe which falls all too often on hard working individuals like you or me. A boss who has a list of names for the next redundancy round in front on them is more likely to choose members of staff that they don't know or don't like over and above a Butt Licker. The simple reason is that Butt Lickers can prove useful, getting things done without question. Once again, the Darwinian survival instinct wields its powerful influence. Butt Lickers are acutely aware that their future depends less on what they know and more on who they suck up to. Incompetent Butt Lickers can outlast even the most competent and politically connected executives because they don't pose any threat.

ANNOYANCE RATING

8 –Butt Lickers are annoying because they are incessant. Whereas we all have to make small talk and compliment our superiors every now and then, Butt Lickers make it their life's work. Never will you hear them say how bad their boss is or what a complete bastard the finance director is. All you hear is a continuous stream of compliments, plaudits, appreciation and recognition for their bosses. Perhaps they have posters of them on their walls at home. Some of the annoyance also stems from the unbalanced opinions, which are always positive. No manager is that respected, liked or competent.

RARITY

4 – There are comparatively few true Butt Lickers around. With so many miserable people at work, few are willing to commit to a life of Butt Licking – unless they are completely stupid, of course.

SEASONAL VARIATIONS

None: I, and indeed my fellow Pain Spotters, have observed very little by way of seasonality in the Butt Licker's behaviour. For them butt licking is a way of life; they are the modern day equivalent of the Knights Templar, a pseudo-religious cult with a sinister undertone. I imagine that they must meet in secret locations to discuss butt-licking tactics and exercise their tongues.

AVOIDANCE/REVENGE STRATEGIES

1. Why not join them? It may boost your career and at the very least should protect you from redundancy.

2. Put a sign up that says "Butt Licking can seriously damage your tongue".

3. Make a trophy in the shape of an arse with a tongue hovering near it and present it to the person who has licked the most butts this year. Better still, why not ask the chief executive to present it?

4. Pose as a researcher who is looking into the effects of excessive toadying on workplace stress and longevity. On completing the research present your findings which recommend that Butt Lickers should be given proper job descriptions and paid more money.

5. Befriend them, take them down the pub, get them drunk and then tie them naked to a lamppost next to the boss's house.

☐ Tick here when you have spotted the Butt Licker

RATE THE
BUTT LICKER'S
ANNOYANCE

The Chimneystack

GENERAL CHARACTERISTICS

There are now over a billion smokers (in Pain parlance, Chimneystacks) in the world clogging up our airways and filling up hospital wards. Fortunately, smoking has been banned in the workplace for some time, but I am sure you can remember when you could light up at your desk, fill the office full of putrid gas, cover your workspace in ash, leave fag ends everywhere and engulf your friends with foul-smelling breath without a care in the world. I really don't care if Chimneystacks want to kill themselves so long as they don't take me with them. It seems that I am not alone, as laws on smoking have changed dramatically. Over the last few years the trend of banning smoking in the workplace has gone global. So our cancer-ridden colleagues are destined to go the same way as the dinosaurs. No more mess, stench, ash and yellow-fingered handshakes. But, hang on a minute: it actually seems that Chimneystacks are the new privileged class.

Let's face it:

- They can take breaks when others can't. With the average Chimneystack puffing away at 14 cigarettes during a working day and each one taking ten minutes, that's over two hours away from work.
- They can hang around the front door dropping fag ends for visitors to walk on. Who needs a red carpet?
- The air always smells fine to them because their noses are clogged full of ash, gunk and all manner of disgusting chemicals.
- They will never become victims of passive smoking.
- They take extra days off sick.

Chimneystacks are a fascination. What is it that makes them take up the habit in the first place? Many do so to be cool with their mates, others say it keeps them slim (I guess cancer does that to you) and a significant number state that it relaxes them, whilst others mention that they love the taste. Have you ever tried French kissing a Chimneystack? Watching them give it up is even better, as they pass through unbelievable mood swings. I heard one story from a non-smoker who worked with a bunch of chain-smoking Chimneystacks. Fags were hanging from their mouths 24–7. The non-smoker would amuse himself in break times by calculating how much of their paltry wage was spent on fags and then telling them how much they could save if they gave up. Some were sufficiently shocked that they did quit. It's also great telling them about the effect smoking has on their body, including all manner of ailments ranging from impotence through to needing a laryngectomy. So the next time you're with a male Chimneystack who tries it on, just respond by asking how it's hanging, or asking "does this banana feel soft to you?"

Chimneystacks come in various shapes and sizes, including:
- **The Bearded Chimneystack.** They usually favour pipes and have telltale yellow stains in their facial hair.
- **The Yellow-Fingered Freak.** Their fingers are so yellow you daren't touch them without surgical gloves.
- **The Rollup.** These people love smoking what look like a tiny pieces of paper that disappear in an instant.
- **The Trendy Tabber.** These people won't actually smoke but will hold their arm out at thirty degrees in an attempt to look cool.

I do love the dedicated smokers' room, where Chimneystacks congregate and see if they can fill the confined space with so much smoke that they need a fireman to guide them back out again. They all traipse in looking despised and rejected, but once in it's a party atmosphere; laughing, joking and enjoying the fact that they don't have to work quite so hard as their non-smoking colleagues. I wish that Sultan Murad IV was still around. He had smokers executed as infidels, with up to 18 a day learning to smoke through man-made holes. But that was almost 400 years ago and we can't behave like that anymore, can we?

ANNOYANCE RATING

9 – Non-smokers detest Chimneystacks with a vengeance. They hate the stink, the squashed butts, the foul breath and ash-infested clothes. There is no doubt that Chimneystacks are the universal hate guys.

RARITY

4 – A significant portion of people still smoke at work although this is gradually dropping as people turn to recreational and hard drugs, which are increasingly cheaper than tobacco. At least they don't smell as bad. Also people prefer to use their mobile phones as the must-have accessory; these days, if you are not seen with the latest 3G videophone between your fingers you're a nobody. As more and more Chimneystacks kick the habit this species of pain will eventually die out.

SEASONAL VARIATIONS

You will see more Chimneystacks in the **summer months** because it's nicer outside. Without smoking rooms or shelter in the winter, cigarette breaks tend to be shorter, but in the summer they can enjoy a bit of impromptu sunbathing whilst having half a dozen tabs. You should also notice a temporary increase in Chimneystacks around **Christmas** when the combination of booze, parties and pheromones lead otherwise sane people to have the odd ciggie or two, if only to impress the opposite sex, or maybe because that will temporarily disable their taste buds so they can get off with the unattractive-looking temp from marketing.

AVOIDANCE|REVENGE STRATEGIES

1. Never sit next to a Chimneystack.

2. Force them to work longer hours to make up for the time they are away from their desk having cigarettes.

3. Spray air freshener around their desks when they come back from their fag breaks.

4. Buy a packet of joke cigarettes and watch them explode as the Chimneystack lights up.

5. Ask if their craving for nicotine is stronger than their sex drive.

☐ Tick here when you have spotted the Chimneystack

RATE THE
CHIMNEY STACK'S
ANNOYANCE

The Company Bike

Although I never grew up in a village, friends of mine who did used to talk about the Village Bike. Being young and naive at the time, I thought they were referring to a collective bicycle used by people in the hamlets in which they lived. Only when I was much older did I realise the full meaning of the term. "Collective" was indeed the word that was most apt, but bicycle referred to a girl in the village who was somewhat free in discarding her knickers. Clearly growing up in a village was more fun than in a quiet market town. Winding forward a few years and into the workplace, what did I find? A new variant of the Village Bike: the Company Bike. The Company Bike is usually, but not exclusively, a female employee who is very free with her body and likes to put it around a bit. They are usually young ladies whose immense charm and beguiling ways are irresistible to their male colleagues. Let's face it, when it is given to you on a plate, the primitive male brain can do little to refuse. Scientists have now confirmed this: apparently, even being shown a picture of a pretty woman seriously hinders a man's ability to make decisions; it fires off neurons in the brain that signal sexual opportunity. The converse is true of women who, when shown a picture of a handsome man, do not change their behaviour in any way. The male response is apparently the same in less intelligent animals; Darwinism in action once again. The Company Bike will drift from one casual one night stand to another, shagging a wide variety of male colleagues, from the very fat to the very ugly. No one seems to mind and if anything the Company Bikes provide some welcome entertainment for the Gossip. There is however a more sinister, or perhaps smarter, genre of the Company Bike: the Career Bike. These are the women (and very occasionally men) who literally sleep their way to the top. The Career Bike is far more discerning than the

Company Bike; they will select only those who can give them that all-important lift to their career. And in the testosterone-fuelled environments in which we now work, who can resist when beautiful young professionals are throwing themselves over you because you have the power that they crave. And remember the research: when facing this situation, you *will* lose control, but let's hope it is not too soon. The Career Bike is less judicious, in that they will sleep with even the most crusty and wrinkly old men in order to get what they want. Perhaps they love the challenge of helping the new, albeit temporary, love of their life to keep it up. Stories of Company and Career Bikes are many and include:

- The hapless accountant who was prepared to offer an investment banker sex in order to get invited to a posh restaurant and have nice holidays. So much for career advancement – the email in which she laid out her sordid plans fell into the investment banker's hands and before long it was winging itself around the world.
- The career-obsessed young lady who would shag anyone to get what she needed. From promotion to overseas secondments, no male decision maker could get in her way.
- Staff from an insurance company sent emails that detailed which Career Bike was sleeping with which boss. The emails were so suitably embarrassing that those identified on the list were overlooked for promotion.

Both the Company and Career Bikes are not for settling down, they will use the men or women around them for either quick flings or as rungs on the ladder of success. Few relish the idea of staying with their latest conquest and would rather move onto the next career-enhancing shag or fun-inducing tryst.

ANNOYANCE RATING

1 – No one likes the fact that a female colleague makes it to the top between her thighs but, judging by a recent poll into sleeping with the boss, it seems that 35 per cent of women would contemplate doing so. More surprisingly, so would 52 per cent of men. Given that most bosses are still male, this is a slightly disturbing result. Amazingly, over 70 per cent of workers under the age of thirty would sleep with their bosses in order to get on. Perhaps, with so many opting this method of advancement, the Career Bike is not such a pain after all.

RARITY

5 – I believe that the Company and Career Bikes are more common than we think. With more and more women entering the workplace and with old men still desperately holding onto their positions, I am sure there are many Career Bikes out there.

SEASONAL VARIATIONS

You will see Company and Career Bikes coming out en masse at **any company party**. It is a veritable London-to-Brighton Bike ride. If you are particularly fortunate you may also spot the Arse Photocopier. These are the people who, having spent their time at the office party photocopying the Company Bikes' arses (and the rest), spend the remainder of the time playing that classic game: "Whose fanny is this?" With a recent survey revealing that 45 per cent of people have had sex at the office Christmas party, this could be a very popular game indeed.

AVOIDANCE/REVENGE STRATEGIES

1. Only work with the old and infirm.

2. Always be wary of anyone offering free sex; there's no such thing as a free munch.

3. Set up a "Tour de Office" competition for all the Bikes, with the winner having the honour of wearing the yellow jersey.

4. Write a book entitled *The Bika Sutra* which details all the ways Company and Career Bikes can get off with their colleagues. Consider illustrating the book and making an accompanying video.

5. Present the Company or Career Bike with a shiny set of bicycle clips for Christmas.

☐ Tick here when you have spotted the Company Bike

RATE THE COMPANY BIKE'S ANNOYANCE

The Competitor

According to the Competitor, second is nowhere. Being number one, top of the tree, pick of the bunch or any other hackneyed phrase is the only thing that is important to them. Everything, and I mean everything, has to be a competition and if it is they must come first. Being top dog is an essential part of their psyche and they will do everything within their power to ensure it remains that way. They are so career obsessed that they give the concept of a career a bad name. They will:

- Put down their competition.
- Lick the butts of those that matter (see the Butt Licker).
- Kick the butts of those that don't.
- Use other people to achieve their ascendancy.
- Know just which buttons to press with their bosses to get their competition discredited by saying things like "I really feel bad about coming to you with this, but Simon is a bad influence in the team and may damage our ability to do a good job for our clients. He's always making bad decisions and we have to pick up the pieces..."
- Sell their children into slavery.
- Sell themselves to fat politicians.

As you would expect, failure is not in their vocabulary because they never see it as their fault, or refuse to do so. They are experts at deflecting blame and responsibility so that even when something goes horribly wrong they walk away from it smelling of roses (they

have learnt wisely from the Teflon and Marigold). One story involved an insidious little man who would always involve his rivals in risky ventures. Although the guy concerned would always lead the opportunity (a great way to suck up to his superiors), if it started to go haywire he would expertly pass the reins to one of his companions. Naively they would see it as a chance to move up the firm and would only realise their mistake when it was too late. They received their ritual drubbing, humiliation and their careers would be put on hold whilst the Competitor's flourished. Before long this Competitor had reached senior management but still continued to use people as means to his ends. Eventually, a group of victims clubbed together and took out an advert in a contact magazine (for those who don't know, these magazines are for making contact with sexually active couples in a particular area) giving the guy's office details. Very soon he was receiving phone calls from a variety of sexual deviants. Competitors are an amalgam of many payroll pains and so tend to get right up their colleagues' noses. Sure, we all accept that there is a degree of competition within any workplace and there are those whose careers are the most important things in their lives, but do we have to endure the narcissistic "big I am" all of the time? Competitors also hate to give anything away. I heard of one guy who was up for promotion and, like all the other candidates, was due to be invited to a meal with the board. When asked about it by one of the other lucky people, he denied all knowledge. Such people are crushing bores because they take their competitive edge to social events too. A friend of mine was even challenged to a lunchtime game of snooker by a Competitor, who happened to lose when he made a foul stroke on the black. Not only did he refuse to acknowledge that he had lost, claiming that a noise distracted him, but he also failed to honour their bet.

ANNOYANCE RATING

8 – No one likes Competitors because they are so obsessed with getting to the top. They are always probing for weaknesses in you and your colleagues' game plans and once these are identified, will exploit them mercilessly. In an increasingly aging workplace you will often hear them say "Oh, you're getting older, I guess it's time to bring in some new blood." They are masters of spin and will take every opportunity to tell you how great they are, how they won the egg and spoon race at their son's sports day and how without them the company would fold. More amusing are the new entrants, and especially the younger ones such as the recent graduates who believe that they are the chosen ones, destined to reach for the sky. Within a few short years they realise that they will never make it and begin to develop their coping strategies to get way with as little as possible like the rest of their workmates.

RARITY

4 – The Competitor is, thankfully, relatively rare. The majority of people at work are foot soldiers, content with getting through the day with the minimum of fuss, effort and hassle. Plus there are so few positions of total power in any organisation that there can only be handful of contenders.

SEASONAL VARIATIONS

The Competitor will always turn up the volume during **promotion rounds** or when there is a career-making project in the offing. You will also see a clutch of Competitors every autumn when the spotty-faced graduates join the company, all believing they are destined for star-spangled careers. It's amazing what people will believe during job interviews.

AVOIDANCE|REVENGE STRATEGIES

1. Stick to working in the post room – you won't find many Competitors there.

2. Ask Competitors if they practice their competitive behaviour on their children.

3. Challenge them to a duel. They can use a sword, you a gun.

4. Scream, shout, and jump up and down and wail "It's not fair, how come you get all the promotions?"

5. Tell them that you know the producer of Superstars and ask them if they would like to take part; when they say yes, give them the number of the local escort agency.

☐ Tick here when you have spotted the Competitor

RATE THE **COMPETITOR'S** ANNOYANCE

The Control Freak

T here are two types of people in this world. Type A and Type B. Those in the former category are driven, need to be in control and can be complete and utter bastards to work for. The people in the second category are laid back, look suspiciously like hippies and can be complete and utter bastards to work for. Bastards aside, of which there are many, there is one pain in the office you really must avoid at all costs and this is the Control Freak (who, as you'd guess, is very much a Type A). As the name suggests, the Control Freak is someone who must control everything, not just the occasional thing but absolutely everything, including you, your work and ultimately the entire business. They see their job as protecting the world against Village Idiots and other incompetents who can't spell their own names, let alone do anything remotely useful at work. Stupid I know, because you can't control people with shit for brains, but then we are dealing with someone who is bit of a baby. You see, a Control Freak is in fact a big girl's blouse, scared of doing anything wrong because they are so worried about slipping up and appearing vulnerable to those around them. I guess their overbearing parents have a lot to answer for. Their response to this deep insecurity is to micro-manage everyone around them. They will constantly badger their staff wanting to know what they have been doing, how they have been doing it and when they will finish. You see, Control Freaks cannot stand it if they are left in the dark. As to be expected, the Control Freak is attracted to certain jobs, such as headteacher, librarian, project manager, accountant, policeman, Sergeant Major and dictator because such jobs offer them the opportunity to control all around them. Dictators are, of course, the ultimate in control freaks, as they want to rule the world. The likes of Genghis Khan, Stalin, Napoleon and Hitler all needed to control

everything and everyone around them. Thankfully, none of them have ever succeeded, but their legacy lives on in all the dictators at work. I was told of a French consultant leading a large engagement with an investment bank. Things were not going well, and the team were up against a tight deadline, which involved getting a report out that evening. She was like a cat on a hot tin roof. She hovered around the team, asking them every two minutes what they were doing and how long it would be before the work would be finished. Everyone was getting mightily pissed off with her constant interruptions. On being asked for the hundredth time "When will you finish?" one guy answered "I don't know, it might be ten minutes, or it might be ten days." She went loopy and demanded to know when the report would be completed to which the chap replied "If you stopped asking me every thirty seconds, I might be able to get my bloody work done!" The problem with Control Freaks is that they just can't let go and they certainly can't cope with leaving anyone else in charge. A close ally of the Control Freak is the Nitpicker, whom we will meet later. I also heard of one Control Freak who would not let his staff apply for professional qualifications unless he wrote their application forms. He would get extremely annoyed and would refuse to endorse their applications if they did the forms themselves.

ANNOYANCE RATING

6 – I guess this depends on where you stand in the organisational hierarchy. Clearly, if you're the boss, having the odd Control Freak around may not be a bad thing. At least they can get things done. But if you are unfortunate enough to work for one, then the misery they cause can be immense. There is nothing worse than having some jumped-up prison guard of a boss or project manager trying to second guess your every move, constantly asking you what you're up to, correcting everything you do and telling you what should have done in the first place. What's more, they usually end up doing your job. The next time they ask you what you're up to, why not say "Mind your own bloody business"?

RARITY

5 – If we assume that half of the working population displays Type A behaviours, then we can safely say that the number of Control Freaks is quite high. But there are certain jobs that will attract more than their fair share of them. For example, I have heard that investment bankers are all Control Freaks, strutting their stuff and shouting and screaming at each other most of the day. Mind you, if you were not one in that job you would probably be sacked. You will see far fewer Control Freaks in other organisations such as florists, refuse collection and sex shops. So if you fancy an easy life, why not avoid the professions that attract such nutters?

SEASONAL VARIATIONS

None; of all the pains, I believe the Control Freak is less controlled by the seasons and mostly driven by the stars. Apparently the Earth signs are the worst (Taurus, Virgo and Capricorn) with their anal retentiveness and obsessive attention to detail. The best way of avoiding these people is to casually ask them about their star sign and when they say they are a Virgo, Taurus or Capricorn, give them a wide berth.

AVOIDANCE|REVENGE STRATEGIES

1. Smile at Control Freaks inanely; this is a sure-fire way to get their blood boiling.

2. Give them some of your Prozac, to which you have become addicted because of their behaviour.

3. Test their blood pressure and give them a lecture on the effects of cortisol and adrenalin on the body.

4. Write them a poem as a way of calming them down.

5. Give them the finger and walk out.

☐ Tick here when you have spotted the Control Freak

RATE THE **CONTROL FREAK'S** ANNOYANCE

The Corrupt Bastard

GENERAL CHARACTERISTICS

orruption is all around us. From Enron-style implosions to the business leaders who line their pockets with more cash and benefits than they could ever hope to spend in three lifetimes let alone one, self-aggrandisement is the order of the day. Everyone is out for themselves. As in nature, this member of the species comes in many different varieties, including:

- **The Super Corrupter.** These are the chief executives who will give themselves outlandish bonuses, share options and pension contributions even when their companies are going down the toilet. In some cases they even pass on some of their ill-gotten gains to their progeny in the form of luxury houses, personal jets and positions on the board.
- **The Pinstripe Corrupter.** These are the city traders who fleece their punters by bamboozling them with jargon and lies so that they can make cash at the expense of their gullible clients. The Pinstripe Corrupter will use techniques such as talking up shares that have nowhere to go but south, conducting bogus trades, hiding losses, and adopting market-timing scams to ensure they can cream off some extra cash.
- **The Charity Corrupter.** A classic Corrupt Bastard if ever there was one. These are the people who will claim to be collecting for the needy when in reality they need it for themselves to blow on prostitutes, hard drugs and luxury holidays.
- **The Professionally-Qualified Corrupter.** These are the supposed professionals who will use their standing to dupe their victims. One story involved an accountant defrauding his company for over £100,000 to fund a prostitution racket.

- **The Brown-Shoed Corrupter.** This is the public servant who embezzles money from us, the taxpayers, in order to provide themselves with a lavish lifestyle that they could otherwise not afford.
- **The Fledgling Corrupter.** Someone who is new to the role and likes to steal the pencils, rubbers, staplers and hole punches from your desk. They may start small, but they are working on breaking into the big time and soon they will be pilfering hundreds of toilet rolls and your expense account.

Of course, given the chance, and the guarantee that we could get away with it, who wouldn't want to add a bit more to their meagre income? I heard of this wonderful story that involved a government employee filling up the boot of his car with all manner of loot from a storeroom which was right in front of the security guards. He did this for a number of years before he was stopped whilst filling his boot for the thousandth time. Further investigation found his house stuffed full of stolen goods. I think he was allowed to keep his job; after all, it is almost impossible to sack anyone in government service these days. I also heard about someone whose uncle worked for a mint many years ago. Whenever he visited his uncle, he would be given a bag of shiny new coins. These coins were always of low denomination (half-pennies, pennies and two pence pieces) and there was always a steady stream. He too was eventually caught. It transpired that he would fill his lunch box with coins every day and once home, would store them in his loft. Only when it collapsed did people get suspicious and after further enquiry he was found to have stolen many thousands of pounds. Other, relatively minor, Corrupt Bastards include one chap who abused the flexi clock and managed to have extra days off work, another who forged a senior manager's signature on his sick notes and a train driver who worked as a DJ when he was supposedly on long-term sick leave. You can't trust anyone these days.

ANNOYANCE RATING

7 – This will vary considerably. I get the feeling that many people accept that corruption is endemic within the workplace and don't get too bothered when a lowly employee on a tiny wage decides to help themselves to half a dozen staples. But people get really annoyed when it is the boss who is at it; of all people, they are the ones who don't need to behave like this because they have millions stashed away already. There seems to be no end of high-ranking Corrupt Bastards who have lavished gifts, cash and property on themselves at the expense of their employees.

RARITY

3 – Thankfully the Corrupt Bastard is quite rare, especially when compared to the number of people in employment. However as more of us see senior managers lining their pockets and celebrity CEOs getting away with it, I am sure more people will turn to corruption to make their lives that little bit more bearable. Although the big stuff is quite rare, I am sure the low-level corruption such as petty larceny, forging sick notes, stealing stationary and so on is as common as dung beetles are around an elephant's toilet.

SEASONAL VARIATIONS

You are likely to spot more Corrupt Bastards around **Christmas**, when the need to get some additional money and presents becomes too much of a temptation to avoid. You may also find an increase in Corrupt Bastards **near retirement** when they realise that they have not saved enough to fund their post-employment lifestyle.

AVOIDANCE/REVENGE STRATEGIES

1. Watch out for the employee who suddenly trades in his Skoda Estelle for a Porsche Boxter.

2. Avoid anyone with eyebrows that meet or tiny eyes.

3. If you suspect anyone is a Corrupt Bastard then grass on them; who knows, if it's someone important you might be able to write a book about it.

4. Place video or web cams around the office to capture the Corrupt Bastard in action.

5. Wear a catsuit, carry a bag with SWAG written on it and see if you can get past security without being stopped.

☐ Tick here when you have spotted the Corrupt Bastard

RATE THE **CORRUPT BASTARD'S** ANNOYANCE

The Diet Bore

I have a simple formula for keeping in trim: Energy in – energy out = fat

It's really quite simple. If you don't want to weigh ten tons, eat less and exercise more. Unfortunately this simple and highly effective formula is lost on too many people. Just look at how many spherical men, women and children there are these days; despite all the warnings we get from the medical profession as well as the nanny state, their girth continues to expand. Of course many of these people could get off their fat butts and work up a sweat but, hey, why do they need to do that when they can just diet? Such people are incredibly lazy because they would rather have some tinpot pseudo-scientist tell them that it's okay to eat a tub of lard three times a day than to put on a pair of running shoes and burn off some of their flab. I call these people Diet Bores. Let's put this into context. There are currently 12 million people dieting in the UK, spending upwards of £2 billion per year on pointless diet regimes. The Diet Bore is someone who has developed compulsive obsessive behaviours around their calorie intake. Diet Bores will talk unremittingly about what they have eaten, the calorific value of the food they have consumed and how much weight they have gained or lost during the course of the last half-hour. Not only that, but they wax lyrical about how eliminating bread from their diet has made them feel so much better and the fact that their stools have turned black and their urine red is actually quite okay. Diet Bores are also exceptionally weak-willed; they are the sad individuals who latch onto whatever diet comes their way in the vain attempt to drop some of their spare tyres. And they will always view celebrity diets with particular fascination: "Oh, I am taking up the celebrity chubby diet and eating nothing but pork rind for the next six months. It's

done wonders, you know, Hollywood swears by it." The fact that it is promoted by some B-rated movie star desperate for some extra cash who couldn't give a tinker's cuss about anyone else's weight has nothing to do with it. The same people purchase every keep fit video by the same celebrities because they think that it will help them shed their excess baggage. The fact that the celebrity has undergone major cosmetic surgery and starved themselves for a month is usually lost on their audience. Diet Bores come in a variety of forms:

- **The Obsessive Atkins**, who will insist on telling you how great it is to eat all the things that are soooo naughty like steak and eggs. They will also inform you how bad carbohydrates are and that you're much better off spooning the residual fat from a roast dinner into your mouth than eating an apple.
- **The Calorie Counter**, who will analyse every piece of food and inform everyone who will listen about how many calories are in particular foods. They will also give you a running commentary on their own daily calorific intake.
- **The Squirrel**, who nibbles away at nuts, rice and seeds whilst working, leaving husks and shells everywhere. I'm sure they are the ones who leave the toilet in such a god awful mess (see the Bowel Mover).
- **The Nightmare Nutritionist**, who will talk with a scientific air about how the alternative foodstuff they are consuming affects the physiology of the brain and "confuses the stomach into thinking it's full".

For years the Diet Bore was the preserve of women. Men, quite frankly, couldn't have cared less about getting fat. However, as men have realised that this lack of interest is causing premature death (along with work, of course) they have taken up dieting with a vengeance. Desperate to make up for lost time, men have taken up the latest diets with equal fervour.

ANNOYANCE RATING

9 – If I have heard one person go on and on about how wonderful Diet X is and how they have lost 1,000 pounds of excess flab, I have heard them all. The Diet Bore is just that, bloody boring and tiresome, change the record, for god's sake; I and so many people have had a bellyful of you describing your diet over and over again. If it's so good, why are you still sporting three double chins?

RARITY

10 – I'm afraid, with the advent of the Atkins Diet, Diet Bores are all around us. But it seems that now the entire food industry has cottoned on to the ridiculous sentiment that it's fine to be lazy and eat more fat than you can shake a stick at. Apparently there are now Atkins-friendly restaurants, fast food outlets and even kebab vans. There are now over 5,000 books on dieting, from the South Sea Diet to the GI Diet, from the Metabolic Typing Diet to the What Colour is Your Diet. But no matter what the diet, you can rest assured that this pain is not only here to stay, but it is likely to grow. The obesity epidemic will ensure that.

SEASONAL VARIATIONS

You will definitely see and hear many more Diet Bores around the **summer** when everyone is desperate to squeeze into their undersized bikinis and posing pouches. This is usually accompanied

by: "We're off to Miami, I've just got to lose some weight." You also find many more Diet Bores **just after Christmas** when, following the consumption of more food than the whole of Sierra Leone, they realise that they have overdone it again. The beginning of the New Year also heralds a stream of proclamations about dieting and the need to lose weight. So predictable.

AVOIDANCE|REVENGE STRATEGIES

1. Spend your time with normal people rather than those obsessed about their diet.

2. Learn to eat properly, take exercise and look trim – then look smug.

3. Share some of the latest research about the detrimental effects of dieting on the body and longevity.

4. Launch a website – diet-bores-R-us.com – and add photographs of the sad dieters in your office.

5. Invent a new diet that consists entirely of cream cakes, chip butties and deep-fried Mars bars. Name it after a neighbour's pet, and spread it around the office by word of mouth. You can then sit back and watch the hilarious consequences with glee as it becomes the latest worldwide dietary phenomenon.

☐ Tick here when you have spotted the Diet Bore

RATE THE
DIET BORE'S
ANNOYANCE

The Dinosaur

GENERAL CHARACTERISTICS

As a child I loved visiting the London museums. There you could see the mummies of Ancient Egypt, the dinosaurs of the Jurassic and plenty of stuffed animals. When I started work a couple of decades later I thought I was back in a museum, as what did I find but a bunch of old farts, all of whom lived in the past and should have been museum pieces themselves. It was only when I was overseas with the Royal Engineers in Kenya that I heard the term "the Dinosaur". The officer who introduced me to it was referring to the Mathaga Club, just outside Nairobi. It was here that all the old colonials would congregate reminiscing about how great it was before self-rule and what fun they had abusing and shooting the "natives". They would also lament the passing of the Raj and other bastions of the British Empire. Having sated their hunger, they would settle back in their opulent armchairs and fall asleep, dribbling like babies until it was time for bed. The Dinosaur is an apt name for those older members of the workplace who refuse to adjust to modern life. Change just passes them by, as do most technological advances. Of course, in the past, Dinosaurs would have been destined for the scrapheap before they had even reached the qualifying age of 50, but in this politically correct and anti-discriminatory age, Dinosaurs are valued members of the working population well into their seventies. The warning signs that suggest you or your colleagues are more like dinosaurs than spring chickens include:

- An obsession with nostalgia typified by going on and on about the good old days when work was easy and the only technology you had to worry about was the internal combustion engine. Dinosaurs also lovingly talk about the War, the Queen Mother and rationing.

- A fear and mistrust of youth highlighted by constant complaining about young people in general. They will often say things like "young people today just don't know how lucky they are... in my day..." It should be noted, however, that when faced with so many young people in the office, some Dinosaurs try to look youthful and behave as though they were still in their prime. I have heard of women in their early 50s compensating for their loss of youth by attempting to pull much younger men, drinking everyone under the table and wearing inappropriate clothes. I guess there is nothing worse than Dinosaurs who can't recognise that they are already extinct.
- A declining interest in personal hygiene exemplified by a stale hum about them, increased dandruff and black teeth.
- A tendency to resemble Victor Meldrew and moan and bitch about everything and anything. For them, complaining begins to become a way of life. Don't confuse them with the Moaner, though, for whom complaining is a profession.
- An increased interest in all things medical which is accompanied by long discussions about their health, piles, pills and what they were laid up in bed with last week.
- Death. Somewhat final, I guess, but one Finnish tax auditor did just that. Apparently he died at his desk and went unnoticed by his colleagues for two days. Even his closest work friends failed to realise he was dead and assumed he was busy working on a complicated tax return.

So, despite what scientists have been telling us about the death of the Dinosaurs, they are alive and well. So much for meteorites.

ANNOYANCE RATING

4 – In the main, the Dinosaur is only mildly annoying. Indeed, as we get older we all start to develop telltale signs of extinction. So there is little point complaining about Dinosaurs because it is only a matter of time before we join them. However, when it comes to introducing radical change or new technology into the office, the fun really starts. They will slow any change programme down to a trickle because they fail to grasp even the simplest of concepts. Although Dinosaurs are not quite as stupid as Village Idiots, it is obvious that the aging process has taken its toll on their grey cells. But, as we all get older, the last thing we want to do is to learn something new; we would rather maintain the status quo. So whenever you are having to implement anything new in the workplace and are surrounded by a bunch of Dinosaurs, you might as well forget it and do something else, like watch Jurassic Park.

RARITY

6 – The number of Dinosaurs is growing steadily. As the working population continues to age and as employees find themselves having to work well into their sixties (mainly because they can't afford to retire), the number of old men and women who harp on about the good old days will undoubtedly increase. Although when I joined the workforce twenty odd years ago there were comparatively few Dinosaurs, by the time I retire not only will there be plenty more, but I'll be one too. I'm looking forward to it.

SEASONAL VARIATIONS

None. Rather than there being any discernable seasonal variations with Dinosaurs, what you will notice is a variation in their numbers. Some of your colleagues will enter the Dinosaur zone, whilst others will leave it for the joy of retirement. It isn't a bad idea to map out the age profile of your office and create age zones. In this way you ought to be able assess the percentage of Dinosaurs in your company whenever you like.

AVOIDANCE|REVENGE STRATEGIES

1. Work in a dot-com where only young people work – oops, most of these have gone the way of the dinosaur already.

2. Dress up as an archaeologist and start digging around the Dinosaurs' desks in the hope of finding something even older and more useless than they are.

3. Film a documentary about ancient people at work and call it the Age of the Dinosaurs.

4. Give the Dinosaur a copy of the cult film Logan's Run, about a society where everyone over the age of 35 had their life "terminated".

5. Invite an undertaker into the office to discuss funeral plans.

☐ Tick here when you have spotted the Dinosaur

RATE THE
DINOSAUR'S
ANNOYANCE

The Distracter

I am sure that the general consensus about open-plan offices is that they are a bad thing. Research has even pointed out that optimum productivity can only be attained when three to four people are locked away in an office together. Too few, it seems, and we all pine for other people's company; too many, and we crave solitude. Unfortunately, the majority of us have to suffer the never ending obsession with open-plan offices (for "open plan" read "cheaper office space") which means that we have to endure all manner of disturbances from the Distracter. Distracters are oblivious to the annoyance they cause; perhaps they are deaf, blind or both; unfortunately most aren't mutes. And, boy, are they irritating. The problem is that in an open-plan office you cannot escape their distracting habits, and before long you become overly sensitised to their grating voices, nervous tics, tapping, shaking coughing, throat clearing, nose picking and aggressive use of office equipment. The principal sub-genres of the Distracter include:

- The Tapper. The Tapper is someone who feels compelled to move various parts of their body continuously in time to some funky rhythm playing in their head. They will tap their fingers on the desk, feet on the floor and even heads on the wall (mind you, I think this type of Tapper ought to be sectioned). The Extreme Tapper is someone who hits the keys of their keyboard so hard that you can hear it from the other side of the office.
- The Foghorn. The Foghorn is possibly the most aggravating member of the Distracter family. The Foghorn is someone who seems to be interminably deaf and hence cannot judge just how loud they are. Either that or they love the sound of their own voice so much that they feel duty-bound to share it with the entire office. It's not just the volume of the Foghorn that is so intensely annoying, however; it's feeling intimately involved

with the mind-numbing conversations they are having with colleagues, their customers or even their goddamn children that drives us round the bend. Here's a plea from your long suffering workmates, turn the volume down!

- The Speakerphoner. This is a truly annoying individual and a very common one, too. What is it with people who insist on putting their phone on speakerphone for listening to their voicemails? Pick the bloody handset up; no one wants to hear you run through your messages. And for those of you who also insist on holding telephone conversations on the speakerphone: please don't. Not only does it sound as though you are talking from the inside of a public toilet, but you also don't impress any of your colleagues who are trying to concentrate on something else.
- The Unspeakable. These are the Distracters who have such disgusting habits that you can't help but do a double take. They are your colleagues who will pick their noses and smear it on the underside of their desks; pop into a cupboard or photocopy room, fart and creep out; bite their knuckles; shove their fingers in their ear to dislodge a particularly stubborn lump of wax and then, before it spreading on their desk, inspect it – and, of course, men who insist on rubbing their groins: not a good idea when wearing white trousers.

I heard of one Distracter who, when sitting down, would bounce his knee up and down so fast that everything around him would vibrate. Now, this might have been great for his female companions (who wouldn't have to resort to the washing machine), but for everyone else it spelt disaster. Not only did his constant trembling put people off, but his knee would knock the table and spill everybody's drinks. By the end of one meeting the table was awash with water, coffee and tea. Then there was a bank employee, an Unspeakable Distracter who would scuttle off to the safe, fart and return to his desk. His behaviour was often augmented by a sly sniff of his sweaty armpits, usually achieved by wiping the palm of his hand between his arm and chest and nonchalantly passing it beneath his nose. Although he hoped no one would see, everyone did.

ANNOYANCE RATING

8 – A lot of people like silence when working. Maybe such people are in the minority, given the prevalence of Distracters, or maybe their hearing is particularly sensitive. But many of the people canvassed whilst writing this book agreed that the Distracter is one of the most hated pains in the open-plan office. Why can't they shut up? And why, oh why, do they have to shout when someone is less than two feet away?

RARITY

8 – Distracters are everywhere and with the current obsession with open-plan offices it is unlikely that they will ever go away. Also, with an aging population we can look forward to many more Distracters with whistling hearing aids as the workforce gradually goes deaf. It won't be long before we'll be clearing up the mess from incontinent staff (indeed, with Unspeakable Distracters around, some of us may already be doing so). That's a distraction that none of us want.

SEASONAL VARIATIONS

I don't believe there is any real seasonal variation in the Distracter's behaviour. They have the power to put you off **all year round.**

AVOIDANCE|REVENGE STRATEGIES

1. Wear dark glasses and earmuffs to eliminate the visual and auditory distractions around you.

2. Smear flour and water paste over the Distracters' speakerphones.

3. Pump white noise through the office so that it cancels out the noise from the Foghorns and Tappers.

4. Cover the desk with thick padding so that no matter how hard the Distracter taps and bumps you won't hear a thing.

5. Club together and buy the Distracter a gift membership to the Noise Abatement Society.

☐ Tick here when you have spotted the Distracter

RATE THE **DISTRACTOR'S** ANNOYANCE

The Early Bird

GENERAL CHARACTERISTICS

The old proverb, "the early bird catches the worm", contains some important advice for all of us. Those of us who are willing to take a risk or two and do something before someone else stand to gain a lot. It seems that this ancient proverb has been taken to heart by a number of people in the office, who will come in very early or stay extra late in order to impress their bosses. I call such pains the Early Bird and the Night Owl. The Early Bird is someone who will get into work before anyone else and position themselves so that they are spotted by their bosses when they appear. The boss, on seeing the Early Bird, will usually applaud their commitment to the firm. The Night Owl is someone who stays late, often much later than anyone else. They will hang around looking busy until all their colleagues have gone. Although everyone knows that they are doing it for show, Early Birds and Night Owls will come out with such statements as:

- "I woke up early this morning, so thought it would be a great idea to get to work… I had nothing else to do."
- "I've got so much to do, I just don't have the time to do it in normal hours."
- "I don't do much in the evenings. It's either carry on working or going to meet attractive women and having a good time."
- "I think it's so important to be committed to your employer."

One story that was told to me related to a contractor working as part of a large team in an insurance company. A small team found themselves up against it and would regularly work all through the night to get the work done. The manager was a complete bastard who

cracked the whip and gave them regular bollockings for not working hard enough. At the same time, there was this consultant who was looking after some trifling part of the project and had every opportunity to work near-normal hours. But no, he insisted on shuffling papers on his desk for sixteen hours a day. He would be in before seven in the morning and would leave at eleven in the evening. Not once did he offer to help out the team who were working their nuts off. During this time he delivered nothing and even had two administrative assistants helping him. Even they couldn't work out what he did all day or how he could fill so many hours. Then there was the boss who insisted on writing the time on his memos (this was before email). The time on each one was always out of standard hours, and usually very early in the morning. It cut no mustard with his boss, who apparently thought the guy was a complete tosser who couldn't do his job properly. Another story involved a guy who habitually worked late. Five nights a week the Night Owl would be the last to leave the office. As expected, his bosses got suspicious and decided to hang back and see what was going on. It transpired that he was downloading porn, burning it onto CDs and selling it over the Internet. It wasn't long before he was sacked.

ANNOYANCE RATING

7 – It wouldn't be quite so bad if all we had to put up with was the Early Bird's strange sense of timekeeping, but it's the comments that come with it. They will say such things as "part-time, are you?" or "half day, is it?" and will also insist on telling you what time they got into the office, or what time they left. For god's sake, no one gives a shit. If you want to impress us, why not put a full day's work into a normal working day?

RARITY

7 – As the world of work gets more competitive, with more of us chasing fewer top jobs, we should expect to see quite a lot of Early Birds and Night Owls. The fundamental problem with this is that it can soon become a bidding war, with each Early Bird getting in earlier and earlier to demonstrate how in love with work they are. And, at the other end of the spectrum, Night Owls staying longer and longer before they go home. Eventually we will see these keen careerists staying at work 24–7. We must also recognise that the long hours culture in the UK and other countries is adding to the ranks of Early Birds and Night Owls. As everyone runs scared of being sacked, they take the conscious decision to work longer hours. It's as if they believe that it will help their case. In reality it doesn't, because they are perceived to be inefficient – plus the bosses hate them anyway. I

just hope they all fly off for the winter and never come back.

SEASONAL VARIATIONS

You will tend to see many more Early Birds and Night Owls **just before the appraisal process** kicks in and especially **before bonus time**.

AVOIDANCE/REVENGE STRATEGIES

1. Give the Early Birds books on time management.

2. Ask them if they are having difficulties keeping up with their workload.

3. Time lock their desk drawers and computer so that they can only access them during normal working hours.

4. Complete a time and motion study in order to highlight how low their productivity is and use this to get them the sack.

5. Reset your laptop's clock then time your emails to colleagues so that it appears you have been working all through the night. You will gain much respect from your fellow Early Birds and Night Owls.

☐ Tick here when you have spotted the Early Bird

RATE THE **EARLY BIRD'S** ANNOYANCE

The Eccentric

GENERAL CHARACTERISTICS

J ust as we saw the Nutter in Pains on Trains, we should expect to see its equivalent in the office. Welcome to the Eccentric. The Eccentric shares many of the characteristics of the Nutter, not least our inability to classify them. What's interesting is that unlike the Nutter, who is beholden to no one, the Eccentric has to remain gainfully employed. As a result, their behaviour is not quite as bizarre. However, I struggle to understand why they remain on the payroll. Examples of the Eccentric include:

* The woman boss who thought it would be highly amusing to distribute porn to her female colleagues and who would regularly leave hard core pornographic images on their desks.
* The group of young to middle-aged men who would congregate in the stairwell of one office in order to practice juggling. Not content with balls, they would use rings, batons and occasionally skittles. Before long they were practicing on unicycles. Why they couldn't do it after work and outside no one knew, especially as this happened to be on a busy corridor.
* The chap who would keep proctologist's equipment in his drawer and then wave it in front of his colleagues (especially the new ones) given half the chance.
* A guy my father-in-law used to work with who was not only unkempt, didn't wash and would often wear odd socks, but also never, ever washed his car; it got so bad that it had grass growing on it. He also worked with another guy who would play the "fartophone" (using his cupped hands and blowing raspberries through them) and entertain his workmates with popular tunes of the day.

- The guy who would come to work wearing a bright red wig and, once settled at his desk, would take it off revealing his shiny bald head. He would place his wig lovingly on his desk, occasionally stroking it as though it was a pet dog. When it was time to go home, he would put it back on his head and walk off.
- The banker who had unhealthy obsession with Dilbert. He would sit at his desk all day surfing the Dilbert website, laughing out loud and then printing cartoons off to give to people. The fact that the guy never did any work didn't seem to bother anyone.
- The thrusting executive who would engage in some very strange behaviours indeed, some of which involved him having sex with his girlfriend, filming it and then streaming it onto the internet. Not content with that, he actually publicised it around the office. He would also spy on his exes by installing sophisticated bugging software on their computers.
- The self-congratulatory jerk who designed his own website in order to influence his bosses. The site, which included testimonials from friends, family and clients, was distributed to all his managers. Needless to say this went down like a lead balloon and, in fact, most people thought it so stupid that they forwarded on to their colleagues to brighten up their day.

I always thought that the culture of an organisation was so strong that such oddities would be snuffed out. But things are changing. With the advent of political correctness (see the Political Corrector) companies have to guard against any form of discrimination which means they now welcome such weirdos with open arms. Apparently they call it diversity. However, there is a positive side, as it is the Eccentric who is often the innovator, creating new ideas and products, something the majority of pains seem incapable of doing.

ANNOYANCE RATING

2 – If nothing else, the Eccentric provides one of the few sources of amusement within the workplace. So we ought to let them off. If you work with them, or perhaps for them, you might have a different view, of course.

RARITY

5- I think you might be astonished at the number of Eccentrics in the workplace. Admittedly, many are hidden away from view, either in dark offices well away from reception, or in Research and Development. You are more likely to spot them in government organisations where they know they can be employed without any need to conform to the usual norms and standards expected in a private business. Similarly, you will find concentrations of Eccentrics within certain functions, like IT, where eccentricity appears to be the norm.

SEASONAL VARIATIONS

The Eccentric may display even more bizarre behaviour **around the festive season** when they are permitted to let their hair down even further than normal. So get your videophone out for some corking pictures.

AVOIDANCE|REVENGE STRATEGIES

1. Only work with sane people... if you can find any.

2. Play the record "They're coming to take me away, ha ha" by Napoleon XIV.

3. Wear a white coat and pose as a psychoanalyst who has been hired by the CEO to investigate strange phenomena at work.

4. Run an Eccentric of the Month competition and dish out badges to the winners.

5. Dye your hair bright purple, wear open-toed sandals with green socks, a yellow shirt, swimming trunks and a crash helmet. You'll feel right at home.

☐ Tick here when you have spotted the Eccentric

RATE THE **ECCENTRIC'S** ANNOYANCE

The Egotist

GENERAL CHARACTERISTICS

If we are to believe Freud, there is something of the Egotist in all of us, and it is at work where our egos can be given their best airing. Egotists are people who have but one love in their lives: themselves. In the same way that Narcissus fell in love with his own reflection, Egotists fall in love with their own accomplishments, status, positions and anything to do with themselves. This is not enough, because they also require constant praise and exaltation from their subordinates and must, at all costs, be in the limelight. They are the David Brents of the real office. To achieve these objectives and defend their egos they will lie, bully, cheat, manipulate, withhold negative information and over-emphasize the positive, take credit and throw tantrums. Indeed, this last tactic is more common than you think. I have heard of many senior executives crying and jumping up and down like spoilt brats when they don't get their way. Just pass them a dummy and give them a swift smack around the ear. That should sort them out. Egotists will surround themselves with Butt Lickers and yes-men and will do their best to undermine anyone who does not wish to sing their praises. They will be particularly concerned about how they are perceived by their superiors and will spend hours crafting their image. They will also worry about their subordinates, but only in order to steal their ideas or use them as scapegoats when things go wrong. It should come as no surprise that their underlings think they are complete idiots. Although not every Egotist is in a senior management position, all will adopt the same strategies.

Egotists like to compensate for their deep insecurities and desperate need for adoration by projecting an inflated sense of self-worth and expertise to everyone around them. Of

course, in order to achieve this they become practised at making those around them look crap. One story told to me by a colleague involved someone being asked by his boss to get him some sushi from his favourite Japanese restaurant. When the chap told his boss that he wasn't in the vicinity of that particular eating house, and in any case had other work to do, the boss laid into him, saying that if he told him to wipe his dog's arse he had to do it. The only choice he had was whether to use tissue or his hands. Needless to say, the sushi soon arrived – but before the bloke gave it to his boss, he spat in it. But it's not just about making other people look bad (in order to make the Egotist feel good), it's also about sounding off the ego foghorns. Telling everyone how great they are is a sure-fire way to get a promotion. If they say it long enough the people that matter might even believe them, even if no one else does. I was told of one consultant who, although thrown off an important client assignment, still claimed that he had not only undertaken his role, but also that he'd run the entire job. He couldn't cope with failure, so he pretended it had never happened and no one questioned him. Telltale signs of Egotists include these:

- They have all their certificates on their office wall, including the ones they got for finishing meals in restaurants when they were kids.
- They will have pictures of themselves everywhere, especially those with celebrities and politicians.
- They will use their speakerphone whenever possible, even though the person they are talking to sits next door.
- They will name-drop and talk about how they lunched with the chief executive.
- They will claim credit for anything that has gone well and nothing that has failed.
- They will threaten anyone who gets in their way.

ANNOYANCE RATING

8 – Egotists are legends in their own minds which makes them incredibly difficult to work with and for. They are one of the many obsessive pains you meet in the office. They will come up with rubbish like "I'm your boss, don't forget it," or "without me, this organisation would have failed years ago." Everyone believes they are jerks except those that matter. The careful grooming of their self-image means that those in charge actually think they add value. Maybe it's because an Egotist provides an accurate reflection of those in authority.

RARITY

6 – As people become more and more insecure – witness the increasing number of us who seek therapy because of the miserable lives we lead – they need their egos boosted. Also, the further up you go in an organisational hierarchy, the greater the number of Egotists.

SEASONAL VARIATIONS

Like many in the workplace, Egotists are especially prevalent during the **end of year appraisal process** or during the promotion round. They also love **Christmas parties**, as this is the time when they can put all their dysfunctional behaviours to the test. From toadying with the chief executive, to walking round with signed pictures of themselves, all their behaviours are nauseating.

AVOIDANCE\REVENGE STRATEGIES

1. Never challenge an Egotist, not unless you want to pick up a huge wedge of cash for constructive dismissal.

2. Ask them if they came from a broken home and whether they broke it.

3. Buy them a mirror.

4. Get a talent spotter to ring them up and ask if they would consider playing the evil queen in Snow White on a run-down pier on the South Coast.

5. Remind them of what happened to Narcissus.

☐ Tick here when you have spotted the Egotist

RATE THE **EGOTIST'S** ANNOYANCE

The Excuse Maker

L et's face it, when your alarm bell kick-starts you from your slumber on a workday morning, the last thing you want to do is to drag yourself into the office. Even the most motivated of employees occasionally think as they wake up, "I really can't be arsed, I think I'll just throw a sickie." According to the latest research, six out of ten of us would. But if that's the case, what will we tell our bosses, who are excitedly expecting us to turn up at 9:00 a.m. on the dot? Now, there are some people who are expert at coming up with a justification, and there are those who are not. The latter are probably just plain stupid, but the former are what I term Excuse Makers. The Excuse Maker has an impressive repertoire of stories that are capable of convincing all but the most able of detectives. They come in a number of guises:

- **The Sickie Specialist**, who will feign illness to get a day off. Given that six out of ten workers take a day off for this reason when there is no illness involved, this is a clearly common form of Excuse Maker.
- **The Doctor Dupers**, who are more sophisticated than Sickie Specialists because of their ability to convince their doctors to sign them off work, usually because of stress.
- **The Post-Party Poorly**, who are so hung over from the previous night's session that they cannot get out of bed, let alone into work.

The Excuse Maker is expert at coming up with reasons for not turning up to work. Like the following (all real, would you believe):

- One man who didn't show up one morning said "The clocks have just changed and it was darker this morning. I was taking my dog for a walk and walked into a telegraph pole".
- One woman would take time off to have sex with her boyfriend, who expected her to travel to him. The first time she used the excuse of moving house and retrieving her belongings from storage. The next time she claimed that her father had just a stroke and was only found out when her supervisor rang her mother to find out how the poor chap was.
- One guy would ring up his employer and claim that yet another relative had died, and he needed to attend the funeral. The amount of times he claimed that his uncle, aunt, father, mother, grandmother and any other relation he could think of died, you'd have thought that he had the world's largest extended family.
- One woman working for a large firm went AWOL and despite every attempt to contact her, no one could track her down. It turned out that she didn't fancy working there any more and went off horse-riding each morning instead.

If you think about it, there are all manner of reasons why you might not make it into work. These range from the obvious ones like colds and flu through to the more credible, like the trains being up the spout (which, of course, they usually are), and the entirely surreal, such as those associated with visitors from out of town and freak events in the home. Clever Excuse Makers will use a range of explanations and rarely the same one twice. The problem comes when they return to work, especially if they have claimed to have been ill. They have to be able to feign the tail-end signs of an illness, or the ongoing feelings of loss associated with a dead relative. This is not always that simple and, unless they are very clever liars, they can often get caught out. Plus, after a while, no one trusts them so they may end up getting the boot for being rubbish at work. Of course, for those readers who are heavily into workstrology, I am sure the stars will provide them with plenty of ammunition. Things like "My stars suggested that something awful might happen at work today, so I stayed in bed," or "My stars recommended I try a new venture today, so I went skydiving".

ANNOYANCE RATING

2 – I don't believe Excuse Makers are really that annoying. If anything, you have to admire their gall and ability to concoct amazingly convincing stories. Perhaps the annoyance rises when you are the one having to pick up the pieces, but in the main, I love to hear the ridiculous stories because they brighten up an otherwise dull day.

RARITY

9 – The Excuse Maker is a very common pain. All of us have made up excuses for not going into work at one time or another.

SEASONAL VARIATIONS

Excuse Makers will undoubtedly make the most of the **winter months** when they can claim to have any number of weather-related illnesses and mishaps. They can also use the parlous state of the nation's railways as a particularly convincing explanation. This ensures they can get some extra time under the duvet. Similarly, **summer** can provide other excuses, such as hay fever, sunburn, heat exhaustion and melted rails. Here the object of the excuse is to get more time relaxing on the sun lounger.

AVOIDANCE|REVENGE STRATEGIES

1. Always get suspicious when someone constantly rings in on a Friday or Monday morning claiming to be poorly. More likely than not, they are throwing a sickie in order to have a long weekend.

2. Ring them up every 15 minutes to see how they are and demonstrate that you are a caring, sharing employer.

3. Keep a log of the excuses used and publish them on a regular basis around the office.

4. Sack your Excuse Makers, so that they won't have to make up any new excuses.

5. Develop some software that produces a random excuse for each day of the week. Ensure that it takes into account the time of year, weather and the family circumstances of the user. Sell it for £10 a copy and watch yourself get very rich, very quickly.

☐ Tick here when you have spotted the Excuse Maker

RATE THE
EXCUSE MAKER'S
ANNOYANCE

The Extracurricular

This is the first entry which describes people who will do their utmost to avoid proper work. At school extracurricular activities were usually quite diverse, and ranged from playing the violin or joining the rugby team to having sex with your teacher. For those old enough to remember, they also entailed delivering warm milk to your schoolmates. This much-cherished job was always very popular because it meant you could avoid assembly. As a result it was usually hotly contested and those who failed to secure the role were scarred for life – rejection starts early. At work, extracurricular activities can be quite similar, but those looking for the sex bit will have to look elsewhere. The Extracurricular is someone who likes to replace mainstream work with other "work" that can be considered to be fun, non-core or in fact anything that adds no intrinsic value to the business. Some roles also provide the closet Nazis amongst the workforce with a chance to reveal their true colours. Take the Health and Safety representative, for example. Their main role is to send out lots of bulk emails to add to the spam that clutters up our inboxes. I guess most men will delete the health and safety related mails and open up the "increase your penis size by 80%" ones instead. The emails from your ever-helpful rep will cover such diverse subjects as not keeping boxes under your desk, not leaving your wet underpants on the printer to dry or testing electrical equipment. No one takes heed of the important messages, so they will come and enforce their health and safety message by offering you advice on how you should sit at your terminal. Other types of Extracurricular include:

- **The First Aider**, who will organise events in which you can set fire to your friends and learn in real time how to treat third degree burns with the minimum of equipment.

- **The Charity Tout,** who will spend lots of time drumming up support for their latest venture. These normally involve some hare-brained scheme such as being shot out of a rocket, abseiling down Angel Falls, lying in a bath of cold baked beans or seeing how long they can keep their head down a flushing toilet. In the process they will get time off work, fleece you of your hard-earned cash, get a holiday and avoid doing some real work for a week or two. Such people are perhaps too good to be true. They are great at making you feel guilty if you are not supporting their worthy cause, but you do have to ask yourself just who they are doing it for.
- **The Events Organiser**, who will waste months organising a party which very few people will attend (unless forced to), and where those who do turn up will probably get pissed, get off with their colleagues, vomit and go home.
- **The Union Rep**, who will go round causing trouble and threatening to strike over every complaint no matter how trivial, like there not being enough Kit Kats in the vending machines.
- **The Coach, Mentor and Counsellor.** These people see it as their responsibility to help staff cope with their terrible working environment and the general futility of employment. They will take you out for coffee to understand what makes you tick, feedback to you your development points and offer advice about your career and future (none, of course). Many have picked up a book on neuro linguistic programming or have seen a motivational speaker and try to emulate their treacly style.

One story involved a Health and Safety rep sending out a particularly lengthy email concerning Christmas decorations. As you'd expect, there were plenty of restrictions ranging from no tinsel around the monitors, through to no standing on chairs or using sticky tape on the walls. The flagrant use of Christmas cards was forbidden. He even guarded the official Christmas tree and would stand over the maintenance men to ensure no illicit fairies appeared and that it conformed to European standards. When a couple of guys went back to this official's house they saw a huge tree covered with cheap lights, wires everywhere, overloaded sockets and endless candles next to flammable material. It's a bit like nurses, who work in such clinical environments that their homes are complete tips.

ANNOYANCE RATING

8 – The Extracurricular is annoying for a variety of reasons. They draw salaries yet add bugger all value to the bottom line. All they do is get in your way, slow you down and interrupt you with pointless requests such as support for the latest charity stunt they are intending to pull off. The next time there is a headcount reduction, these are the people who should be offered the loaded gun to place at their temples.

RARITY

4 – Thankfully, there are comparatively few Extracurriculars. In most offices they are usually restricted to those who dream of having power but are generally incapable of achieving it by any other means, or people who feel it is an essential part of their job to save the world on the company's time.

SEASONAL VARIATIONS

This very much depends on the type of Extracurricular you are dealing with. Those organising charity events will tend to surface during the **summer months**, whilst the party organiser will focus their efforts **around Christmas** and colleagues' birthdays. You will also see more of the Health and Safety rep at Christmas too.

AVOIDANCE|REVENGE STRATEGIES

1. Never comply with any edicts that emanate from an Extracurricular. If enough people ignore them, maybe they will just go away.

2. Place a notice above your desk saying "No hawkers, beggars, or closet extremists".

3. Ask the boss to ban all extracurricular activities which take place in company time.

4. Set up a protest group who will take any topical issue and march through the office with placards. You can march about animal rights, student poverty, global warming and all manner of issues. In fact, there is so much to march for that there won't be any time to do any work.

5. Print a prospectus in the same way local councils do for adult education, which lists all the extracurricular activities that staff can enjoy. Make sure you provide a brief description of the activity, how much time it would take them away from their day job, and a contact number where they can get more details.

☐ Tick here when you have spotted the Extracurricular

RATE THE **EXTRA-CURRICULAR'S** ANNOYANCE

The Fad Surfer

M anagement gurus and MBA students have provided us with a wealth of theories, strategies and models with which we can transform the business using breakthrough techniques, tools and methodologies. The trouble is that all of this is complete bollocks. Anyone who believes the tripe that is peddled out from holders of MBAs, gurus and the other purveyors of snake oil has been caught by one of the most common pains on the payroll: the Fad Surfer. The Fad Surfer is someone who takes great pride in riding the latest wave of management theory. They will mount their beautifully waxed surfboards and swim out through the vast tomes of management bullshit to catch the latest, and hopefully greatest, fad on which to make their fortune. The Fad Surfer has some especially irritating traits including:

- The total conviction with which they proclaim that the latest rubbish coming out from business schools will transform the workplace once and for all. Let me tell you something you already know – nothing really changes and in the majority of cases the latest theory is merely a remould of what was served up to the last generation.
- Their ability to jump from one fad to another without any apology or comeback for the disaster left in the wake of the previous fad that they recommended.
- The insulting way they hope to bring everyone on board by presenting the idea in a wacky and fun way. For wacky, read puerile and for fun, read insultingly shite.

I am sure you have been through many fads in your time. I heard of one example from the height of the dot-com bubble. The person concerned was working for a management

consultancy who were very worried that they would miss the lucrative wave known as the New Economy. No more bricks and mortar, the future was Eeeeeeeee. So the staff had to attend a one day e-immersion course at which they learnt jack shit, were communicated to by an enormous animated frog, played pointless games with a bunch of actors and listened to their leaders tell them how vital all this trivia was. At the end of it they were all meant to be e-consultants. The crash came, the e-consultants were cast off into cyberspace to pursue other interests in the physical world, and everyone went back to the way they had been a few short months before. Government is no better. The drive to e-government has pretty much been a complete waste of money (ours, in fact). So much for having 100 per cent of government activity in e-space, it's still firmly positioned in the waste of space. Then there was the Total Quality Management fad in which great tranches of sane human beings were patronisingly told what a graph was and how important Pareto analysis was to their jobs. Did quality change a thing? I don't think so. Time and time again we are subjected to the Fad Surfer's obsession with the new. We have had self-managed teams, MRP, ERP, CRM, BPR, TQM, Six Sigma, MBO, ABC, 123, you love me, and so on, and so on. Then, not satisfied with the fads themselves, their creators will turn their hands to writing stupid books about leadership. You know the sort, leadership lessons of Shakespeare, Jesus, Elizabeth I or, god forbid, some bloody cartoon animal. I would like to see Shakespeare run a multibillion corporation with a few impenetrable scripts. To address the scourge of the Fad Surfer, one group of young executives decided to play bullshit bingo at a meeting they had to attend. Everyone was issued with a card which contained a number of common bullshit management words like empowerment, synergy, synchronicity, teamwork, win–win, ballpark, bandwidth and so on. As their leader disgorged one bullshit term after another, the young wags furiously crossed off the words. Competition was hotting up with a couple of the guys neck and neck, then as the last word was crossed off they both stood upright and shouted in unison "Bullshit!" Needless to say their boss couldn't see the funny side. But then they never do.

ANNOYANCE RATING

7 – I'm afraid fad surfing is similar to the Ebola virus; once it takes hold there is little that can be done to save the victim. Plus, it's not much fun. If what they say is true, that bullshit baffles brains, the Fad Surfer is surely a master practitioner. I would go so far as to say that the Fad Surfer probably has shit for brains.

RARITY

9 – The Fad Surfer is incredibly common as business schools churn out more MBA-wielding executives than the Ford production lines do cars. If you ask any young business man or woman what they would like for Christmas, most would respond "I hope Santa brings me an MBA." I think everyone else would rather they got a lobotomy.

SEASONAL VARIATIONS

You will undoubtedly see many more Fad Surfers in the **autumn** when the business schools spew out the latest clutch of masters of the universe. All hope to recoup the huge debts they have run up to learn the ins and outs of globalisation, centralisation, specialisation and, of course, Americanisation. Each and everyone of them will tell you how useful their course has been and how vital it is for your company to embrace the latest management thinking. Give them a few short months in any politically charged, backstabbing corporate environment and they will be talking about starting a media studies course. It's cheaper and at least they will be able to talk with authority about *Pop Idol* without getting their heads kicked in. Well, maybe not.

AVOIDANCE|REVENGE STRATEGIES

1. Avoid anyone who foams at the mouth whenever management theory is mentioned.

2. Play bullshit bingo at key launch events and offer a cash prize.

3. Buy surfboards so that the Fad Surfers can catch the next wave.

4. Tell them to shut up and get on with stacking the shelves.

5. Write a best selling book entitled *Treating Staff Like Slaves: What we can Learn from the Roman Empire* and pass slavery off as the latest management theory.

☐ Tick here when you have spotted the Fad Surfer

RATE THE
FAD SURFER'S
ANNOYANCE

The Flash Git

There are many boring people on the payroll. Some will suck the very life out of you like the Great Bore of Today and the Diet Bore. Others will drive you up the wall like the Tree-Hugger and the Mental Masturbator. But the one that probably caps them all is the Flash Git. Every workplace has them and some professions, such as investment banking, seem to attract more than their fair share. The Flash Git is someone who insists on telling everyone how wealthy they are by throwing the odd comment into their conversation that alludes to their financial position. They are a fine example of our Darwinist tendencies. In most organisations, Flash Gits usually stick out like sore thumbs. They will:

- Discuss their holiday arrangements, which must be exclusive and, of course, expensive. Instead of camping two miles outside Skegness in some dank, miserable shithole of a campsite, they will be dining out under the stars in the Maldives with some half-naked, buxom supermodel.
- Shout across to their secretary such things as "Pop my Porsche in for a service, the number plate is FLASH GIT 1". The fact that the poor secretary is driving a Skoda means nothing to them, naturally.
- Tell you that they haven't got time to meet you at noon because they are picking up an Armani suit from Bond Street.
- Parade around the office in their new designer outfits and handmade shoes.

They play a game focused primarily on what they earn and what trappings they have. I heard of one poor consultant who was working in the city with a client who was a bit of a

game show host. You know the sort, a sleazeball who wore shiny suits, was superficial, had a wafer-thin personality and who, quite frankly, was rubbish at his job. What he did have was a large income. Every day he would call the consultant up from his room with such urgency that you thought he was having a heart attack. When the consultant entered his room, panting from the dash he had just made across the office, he would say something like "Have you seen my new house? It's in the latest edition of *House and Garden*". He would insist on showing the poor chap his bathroom suite, his new Harley Davidson and whatever other tripe he wasted his money on. The Flash Git is insecure and lacks self confidence. The only way they can derive any pleasure is through what they own and the only people who suck up to them are those who are taken in by their grandiose and celebrity-like lifestyle. Most are hollow, sad, lifeless individuals. There are, of course, those people who aspire to becoming Flash Gits, but cannot hope to achieve it through normal means. Some will steal their way to fund the lifestyle to which they aspire and are closely related to the Corrupt Bastard. There was a personal assistant in an investment bank who managed to steal £4.5 million to fund her spending, which included sports cars, holiday homes and Tiffany jewellery. What was bizarre about this case was that her bosses, who earned so much, took ages to realise that they were being stitched up; apparently they failed to miss the cash because for them it was loose change! Then there are the fantasists who live their lives through lies and stories designed to hide their pauper-like existence. One story retold told to me by a secretary involved a previous flame who spun a yarn that he lived in exclusive abodes, drove sports cars and worked in a top organisation. When she was picked up in his car, it soon became apparent his life was somewhat ordinary. He made some weak excuse about his car being in the garage, his house being renovated (which explained why he was living with his mum) and only having to work when he felt like it. Needless to say, she didn't spend much more time with him.

ANNOYANCE RATING

10 – The Flash Git is just that, a flash git. Nothing in their life matters more than having money and the overpriced goods and services that this can buy. They are obsessed with displaying their wealth. They must have the biggest house, the most expensive car, the most bespoke suit and, of course, the trophy partner.

RARITY

7 – The Flash Git is surprisingly common and despite the fact that the rich are getting richer and the poor poorer, there seem to be a growing number of them. Most, I believe, are funding their obsession about being an achiever with equity withdrawal and credit cards. When interest rates rise you will soon see them swapping their BMWs for public transport and their five-bedroom mansions for sheltered accommodation.

SEASONAL VARIATIONS

The Flash Git loves to rub it in at every opportunity, but there are times in the year where they will ramp up their boasting. In particular, you tend to find their unbearable one-upmanship accentuated **prior to the summer holidays** when they can describe their all-inclusive breaks in immense and awe-inspiring detail.

AVOIDANCE|REVENGE STRATEGIES

1. Only work with poor people.

2. Dress up as a priest and say "It is easier for a camel to pass through the eye of a needle than for a rich man enter the kingdom of heaven." I'm sure it will make sod all difference, but it might make you feel a whole heap better.

3. Create a fake film-star lifestyle so that you can outdo the Flash Git. Better still, why not steal money from your employer so that you can fund it?

4. Pour sugar into the petrol tank of their sports car.

5. Mock-up a game show called *Flash Git Extravaganza*. Wear a sequined suit and invite the Flash Gits to compete for exclusive prizes, like the key to the executive rest room.

☐ Tick here when you have spotted the Flash Git

RATE THE
FLASH GIT'S
ANNOYANCE

The Gooser

Why do men believe they have the god-given right to view women as sex objects? And why do they feel that women at work are fair game? Perhaps it's Darwinism. Perhaps it's a power thing. Or perhaps it's because they are Goosers. The Gooser is someone with an unhealthy interest in women, from touching them up as they walk past to making risqué comments about their sexuality, which normally involves some statement about having sex with them. We must of course distinguish between those women, such as the Company and Career Bikes, who will actually seek out the attentions of such people and the majority who come to work to earn a living and don't want to be pestered by perverts. They get plenty of that on the train in the morning. The Gooser comes in a number of different forms, all of which are equally pathetic and each of which shares the common trait of never having sex – well, apart from with their right hand or when they pay for it. The worst kinds of Gooser are:

- **The Dirty Old Man**, who because of his age probably cannot have sex any more. That doesn't stop him trying to chat up all the young women in the office. He will drape himself over their desks, follow them to the coffee machine and generally make a nuisance of himself. The Dirty Old Man is a master of sexual innuendo and when confronted will state that he is only being friendly. Pathetic behaviour for a sad, old, impotent man.
- **The Pumped-Up Prat**, who is usually a youngish executive who has no real outlet for the excessive amounts of testosterone pumping through his veins. He will go around the office making out as though he is some kind of babe magnet, when in fact everyone thinks he is a jerk.

- **The Fast-Fingered Feeler**, who is often middle aged and skilled at touching up his female colleagues. He will brush his hands across the women in his office as he reaches over to pick up a stapler or as they pass his desk. Such people are especially bad at parties, where they will try to touch up every woman they pass.
- **The Brown Mac Misogynist**, who hates all women and likes to make it known. They probably still live at home with their overbearing mothers, who they are secretly in love with. In fact, this is why they hate women so much. They normally own brown macs which get plenty of use in the seedy back streets of Soho and when they are out alone in secluded woodland (see pains in public).
- **The Slimy Sexist,** who loves to make sexual remarks to women in the office and tell offensive jokes. They generally make their female colleagues feel uncomfortable and will make comments like "whilst you're down there, love…" when a woman bends down to pick something up.
- **The Never-Gonna-Get-It Neanderthal.** These are the desperados in the office who, by dint of their general ugliness and lack of social skills, are unattractive to all women. They would love the chance to get their rocks off with one of the female staff but, no matter how hard they try, this never comes to pass. They are better off trying it on with an aardvark.
- **The Excessive Executive**, who believes it is his right to use his position of power in the organisation to goose up any of the female staff. Few can resist his advances because they know the consequences.

As well as sharing a general dislike of women, each type of Gooser shares common attributes. Most are lonely, either living alone in a bachelor pad, at home with their parents or in a loveless marriage. They have such badly honed wooing skills that they could never hope to court even the most tolerant of women. They view women as sex objects and feel threatened by their female colleagues because they realise that they will be exposed as being incompetent, inferior and, of course, impotent. The only way they feel good about themselves is to take it out on the women in the office.

ANNOYANCE RATING

9 – Understandably, the Gooser is particularly annoying to women. It's also unacceptable to men too, who find the Gooser's archaic attitudes and behaviours towards women somewhat depressing.

RARITY

8 – With a greater number of women in the workplace, the opportunities for the Gooser to ply his trade have increased significantly. A lot of men just can't cope with having the opposite sex in the office because it stops them from behaving like overgrown schoolboys. Equally, many cannot stand the fact that there are smarter women than them and on that basis alone we ought to see plenty of Goosers around. There is no doubt that you will see many more Goosers in investment banks and any male-dominated, testosterone-fuelled organisation.

SEASONAL VARIATIONS

There will be plenty more Goosers around in the **spring** when they come out from hibernation. With their sap rising they can't control the urge to touch up the women around the office. You will also find many more Goosers during **any office party** when alcohol turns even the most mild-mannered man into a pervert.

AVOIDANCE|REVENGE STRATEGIES

1. Only work with men who are capable of treating women with respect.

2. Women could try wrapping barbed wire around the key parts of their bodies so that the next time a Gooser "brushes past" they'll get their hands lacerated.

3. Start ridiculing their sexuality by questioning their ability to keep it up.

4. Get a bunch of women from the office to start touching the Goosers up and making fun of the male sex, and see how they like it.

5. Put their genitals through a mincer.

☐ Tick here when you have spotted the Gooser

RATE THE **GOOSER'S** ANNOYANCE

The Gossip

P sychological theory tells us that gossiping is essential to our general well-being, helps facilitate relationship-building, aids group bonding, allows us to clarify social standing, reinforces shared values and ensures conflict is resolved. Blimey, try telling that to someone who has just found out that they are the butt of everyone's jokes about who's sleeping with the photocopying clerk. The term, which originated in Old English, referred to a woman's close friends who were present at the birth of their children; over time it transformed into the activity of sharing intimate details of personal matters and relationships. Darwinism looms large here, as in the dim and distant past gossip was essential to survival. A person's reputation and weaknesses were passed from person to person and it was this word of mouth that determined someone's fate. Anyone who didn't partake in the tittle-tattle was excluded from everything, including sex. Even in this technologically complex age we still love gossip, whether it is about the latest celebrity affair, divorce or court case. Digging up and spreading the dirt is one of our favourite pastimes. The Gossip will target:

- The serial shaggers who can't keep their genitals in their pants.
- The amoebas who are incapable of doing anything, let alone doing it right.
- Anyone who is too ambitious.
- Those who are seen as a threat to their positions or careers. For example, the Competitor will use gossip as part of their armoury to get to the top.
- In fact, everyone.

Of course companies are their own worst enemies. The grapevine is often the only way that news about what's happening gets round. All too often the staff know about the latest round of redundancies before the chief executive announces them. One company was so concerned about gossiping that it set up a helpline for staff to ring to find out what was "really" going on. Surprise, surprise, no one rang. They all preferred to find out the truth from those around them rather than the propagandist tripe peddled by someone from Human Resources. Years ago, the grapevine was controlled by the tea ladies who would wind their way through office corridors picking up all manner of dirt and snippets of information about the company. As part of the service they would dish out the latest gossip along with a cup of hot steaming tea and a biscuit. If you needed to know anything, all you had to do was ask the tea lady. Gossip costs businesses hundreds of thousands of pounds a year as staff "network" to find out what people are saying about each other. It's a damn sight more interesting than work. According to research, some people spend up to six hours a day gossiping, so the Gossip also becomes the Idle Git. There is an interesting side effect in gossiping, known as the boomerang effect. It seems that if you spend all your time gossiping about other people their attributes get transferred to you. Apparently this is the "it takes one to know one" playground retort. So the next time you gossip you might want to say "You know Peter, he is such a great guy, clever, smart, well groomed… this guy is going all the way." Before you know it, you'll be the chief executive.

ANNOYANCE RATING

4 – We all love to hear about the people we work with and we also enjoy spreading rumours about so and so who is shagging Jane in accounts. If nothing else, it adds some colour to an otherwise grey environment.

RARITY

10 – The Gossip is incredibly common and we are all gossips to a lesser or greater degree. There is no doubt that advances in communication technology have increased the prevalence and scope of the Gossip. Over 35 per cent prefer to use the phone and over 20 per cent like to text their gossip. But, let's face it, most prefer to do it in person, if only to see the reaction on the recipient's face. Although both men and women gossip, it is women who believe it is an obligation and god-given right – but then, men don't call it gossip, they call it networking.

SEASONAL VARIATIONS

Gossips will never rest, particularly if they are working in a large company. But it is likely that their activities will increase nearer to **Christmas**. Christmas parties provide the Gossip with the best opportunities to stock up on new stories. The Gossip levels increase hugely the day after a party, as this is when all the "who was sleeping with who" news comes out: "Oh, you'll never guess who shagged Sandra last night, only the CFO! You mustn't tell anyone." Before you know it, everyone knows. Training courses also provide a fertile ground for the Gossip as, just as at the Christmas party, work colleagues can't keep their hands out of each others underwear.

AVOIDANCE|REVENGE STRATEGIES

1. Never gossip (well, try and keep it to a minimum at least).

2. Remember that whatever you say will be repeated.

3. Always be wary of anyone who says they won't tell anyone else. They're basically admitting that whatever they are told will be too juicy for them to keep to themselves.

4. Install a wooden fence between people's desks so that they can lean over and share the latest tittle-tattle with their neighbours.

5. Design a drinks machine that provides similar gossiping skills to a tea lady.

☐ Tick here when you have spotted the Gossip

RATE THE **GOSSIP'S** ANNOYANCE

The Grass

GENERAL CHARACTERISTICS

No one likes a Grass. In the underworld such people find themselves without their kneecaps or swimming with concrete boots in some nearby canal. The Grass in the workplace is equally hated, although in this case they normally escape with their lives: unfortunately. But, rest assured, they will be made to suffer. The Grass, as you would expect, is the antithesis of the Corrupt Bastard. The Grass is usually someone who is obsessed with morality, equality and doing the right thing. They are the morality police, the bottom police, in fact, the anything police. The Grass loves to be able to point the finger at someone and say "nah, nah, nah, nah, nah, I'm telling, sir!" They are identical to the playground snitches who were never prepared to stick up for themselves, instead running to the dinner lady at the first sign of trouble. Don't get me wrong; I am sure there are instances when someone in authority needs to know about major misdemeanours, but in the end everyone hates a telltale. In the same way that the Corrupt Bastard evolves from low-level stealing to international fraud, the Grass will start small and end big. Their evolutionary path is as follows:

- They are born as the **Creep**. Such people don't feel capable of rocking the boat too much, but are willing to dob on their colleagues to their fellow workmates. Small-time stuff, but a sign that they are on the way to great things.
- After a few years as Creeps they will hone their skills and grow into **Snitches**. The Snitch is someone who will grass up their fellow wage slaves to a middle manager. Their physical appearance also begins to change and they start to resemble a weasel.

- The next stage in their evolution is the **Grass** which, for many, is the apogee of their dobbing career. Such people will spend their working day looking for people to grass up, from colleagues who make an inhuman stench in the toilets, to those who have left their PC on all night without password protection. Such people are friendless and often evolve further into the Political Corrector (see later).

- The penultimate stage in their evolution is the **Super Grass**. These are the people who, through religious and moral conviction, will expose their employer to the press and the authorities. One might argue that such people provide an important service for the little people. You might also argue that they are attention-seeking telltales.

- Thankfully few evolve into the worst kind of Grass – the **Celebrity Grass**. This is typically someone who hasn't got their own way and decides to write a book grassing up their company. They always claim that they are doing it in the public interest, but in reality they are out to make as much cash as they can, as quickly as they can. Most were loyal employees who, for whatever reason, were found out to be crap at their jobs or were taken out by internal politics, and none of them have any other motive than to make money out of the process. From writing about how rubbish airlines are to exposing deficiencies within government agencies, all share the same avaricious greed as the Corrupt Bastard. If not, why is it that they have to publish their books around Christmas? If it was such an important issue these could be brought out at any time. Being a victim clearly sells books, but the Celebrity Grasses would do better if they came clean and accepted that all they wanted to do was make a fast buck.

I heard of a Super Grass who, in one heated debate during a project steering committee meeting – which involved ten other people – was not getting his way. He started to shout, then he screamed and finally banged his fists on the table. At the end of this he ran out of the room shouting as he went that he was going to tell Richard what was going on. Although the Super Grass and Richard (a Bully) were lovers, he didn't get his way; well, not in that project at least.

ANNOYANCE RATING

8 – Grasses will always rate highly in the annoyance stakes because they will never be part of a team. They are the schoolchildren no one liked, the last people to be picked from the football line, always standing on the edge of the playground looking dejected and forlorn. They learned that survival meant grassing people up so that they would somehow appear useful to those in authority. Such playground antics have been carried into the workplace where they can wreak far more damage.

RARITY

4 – There are comparatively few Grasses and even fewer Super Grasses in the office. But watch out, as more and more people become disgruntled at work and feel they are not getting their way, the numbers are sure to rise. And with payouts from industrial tribunals increasing, who can blame them? One short court case and they can make more than a year's salary.

SEASONAL VARIATIONS

Although the Grass is with us **all year round**, the Celebrity Grass is highly seasonal. You are likely to spot more of them between September and December when they will be making public appearances to promote their sorry tales of woe in time for the Christmas shopping season.

AVOIDANCE|REVENGE STRATEGIES

1. Always be wary of someone who is taking more than a keen interest in your work.

2. Watch out for people who insist on keeping a diary at work.

3. Hire a private detective to dig up some dirt on the Grass and then blackmail them.

4. Leave a freshly cut square of turf on their desks.

5. Kill them.

☐ Tick here when you have spotted the Grass

RATE THE **GRASS'S** ANNOYANCE

The Great Bore of Today

GENERAL CHARACTERISTICS

It's lovely to hear about other people's experiences. You know, what they have done in their lives, where they have been, what they have achieved and so on. It's the sort of thing that connects people together and makes work that little bit more bearable for us all. What I especially love to hear about are those things that I have never done and perhaps never will, as this can open up new vistas and potential new things to do. But I have seen the dark side, occupied by the Great Bore of Today. The Great Bore of Today is the person who will always have a story better than yours, an experience more exciting, or a tale that is ten times more interesting. They will know more important people than you, and no matter what you have ever done in your life they will have done it as well. We saw the Social Climber in Pains on Trains but the Great Bore of Today is far worse. They have a larger audience and more time to tell the world just how wonderful they are. The Great Bore of Today has a number of sub-genres that we are all too familiar with, and which are too numerous to list here. But here a few:

- **The Billy-No-Mates** who by virtue of having no friends and no life will invent all sorts of incredible stories to match and exceed yours. They are very closely related to the Fantasist whom we will meet later, when I introduce the Liar.
- **The Name Dropper** who will tell you over and over again how they met Lady Di once or how they have been invited to dinner with Lord and Lady Such and Such. Their lives read like an edition of *Hello*, but without the cheesy pictures. Is it possible that these famous and important people are on first name terms with the jerk standing before you? I doubt it. Even if they have met someone famous do you really think they'll remember? In any case no one gives a shit, they just think the Name Dropper is lying anyway.

- **The Proud Parent.** These people live their lives through their kids. They go on and on about what little Johnny is doing, how clever he is and how they want him to go to acting school because he is soooo talented. Poor little sod, all he wants to do is pick his nose and sit around playing games on his PS2. The Proud Parent will insist on telling you about what each of their kids is doing and how clever, talented and – if older – well paid they are. Push, push, push. For proud parent read pushy parent, or indeed crap parent. You see, many of these Proud Parents have such empty, lonely lives that they have nothing better to do than to force their progeny into a succession of Herculean tasks and after-school activities. In reality, this absolves them from doing the job themselves because they are so rubbish at it
- **The Property Bore** who will tell you how important it is to get onto the buy-to-let market and how great it is because you can make so much money. They will wax lyrical about how it's going to be their pension. As rank amateurs, they will be living in a cardboard box when the crash comes.
- **The I've already Done It** is probably the most annoying of the lot. This is the person who has always done exactly what you have and will say "Oh yes, when I went to Hawaii I stayed in this exclusive resort," or "I remember parachuting, in fact I was in the UK team." Their task in life is to outdo everyone else. Of course when you look at them, you can see they have probably never done any of the things they claim to have.
- **The Holiday Bore** who loves to inform you of their next major trip, be it a round-the-world tour, a cruise or two weeks in the Seychelles. They have to tell you about it before they go and after they come back, and if you're really unlucky they will send you a postcard too. What makes this whole experience so awful is that you have nothing better to look forward to than two weeks in a dingy bed and breakfast.

The Great Bore of Today will leave you wishing you had never opened your mouth. What you must get expert at is waiting for the "Ah, of course…" as this should be the alarm bell, your cue to remember that meeting you have to attend or the call you must make.

ANNOYANCE RATING

8 – I guess we hate the Great Bores of Today because they never allow us time to tell them about our experiences. They have this irritating tendency to interrupt our stories before we've really had time to get going. And then, having butted in, they will continue in a tedious monotone without drawing breath. Of course, after a while no one will talk to them, but that doesn't stop them from trying to engage people in the first place.

RARITY

10 – Because every one of us is desperate to be loved by those around us, I believe that we are all bores at some time or other. We need to connect, so we'll tell people about ourselves, our hobbies and what we love to do. Most people will feign interest but the art is to avoid being tiresome. Unfortunately most people fail to do this because they are in essence so egocentric that they can't see that you are dropping off. In conclusion, everyone has the potential to become a Great Bore of Today.

SEASONAL VARIATIONS

There will be the obvious changes in the Great Bore of Today's behaviours such as around the **summer** time, when they will be trekking off to some far flung destination. But there are more subtle ones, such as the New Year's Honours Lists, film premieres and major events in the social calendar, such as Glyndebourne, Wimbledon and Badminton.

AVOIDANCE|REVENGE STRATEGIES

1. Wear some ear plugs and every now and then say "really" in an earnest and fascinated way.

2. Yawn uncontrollably as the Great Bore of Today drones on. When they ask what's wrong, tell them you are suffering from bilharzia which you contracted whilst marching barefoot across a Central African river basin.

3. Hold a mirror up to them and see if they can bore themselves to death.

4. Leave brochures for exclusive holidays and expensive products lying on your desk.

5. Make up the most outlandish story you can and wait for them to come back with the classic "yeah, I remember when…"

☐ Tick here when you have spotted the Great Bore of Today

RATE THE **GREAT BORE'S** ANNOYANCE

The Idle Git

elegation is an essential skill in the workplace. Come to that, so is work. But there seem to be a large number of people out there who have made it their aim in life to do as little as possible, either through expert delegation or the carefully honed skill of looking busy but doing absolutely nothing. Welcome to the Idle Git. The Idle Git is an aficionado of inactivity who has never quite understood the philosophy behind the Protestant work ethic. They come in a variety of forms, including:

- **The Man with a Purpose.** These people rush around the office with papers in their hands looking incredibly busy and stressed out. When asked anything they will always respond "can't stop, off to a meeting..."
- **The Deep Thinker.** They give the impression that they are trying to solve some complex business problem and should not be disturbed.
- **The Arch Delegator.** These people push all of their work onto their subordinates so that they can spend a day on the golf course "networking" with important clients.
- **The Phantom Filer.** They will place all their work and important papers in a filing cabinet elsewhere in the office and pretend that they have completed their tasks.

The strategies the Idle Gits adopt are all designed to shield them from probing questions from their bosses so that they can spend the majority of their day on the phone to their friends and family, running their own business in office hours, rearranging their electronic diaries, taking long coffee and lunch breaks, and generally skiving. Such idleness has been reinforced by a recent survey that suggests that the average worker spends five hours a

week planning holidays, buying goods over the Internet or flirting with colleagues. I heard of one guy who joined a project as software coder. The chap concerned made his way around in an electric wheelchair which made this awful whirring noise. Every day the project manager would set him a task and he would say "yeah, got it, no problem". He would then sit at his desk with his hands on his chin staring out of the window (admittedly there were great views). When quizzed on how well he was getting on he would respond "yeah, fantastic!" In actual fact, he had done sod all. This went on day after day for many months. Once a week the project manager would take him into an office to ask him if anything was wrong. Nothing ever came out from the meetings and the coder continued to stare out of the window. Whenever the project manager heard the noise of his wheelchair, his heart would sink. Eventually he managed to palm him off onto some unsuspecting colleague and he was free. Another story involved an Idle Git who had a scam with a friend who would regularly ring her up and pose as someone from an alarm company telling her that her burglar alarm had gone off. That was the last you saw of her for that day. One of the worst examples I heard of involved an entire office. The office concerned received thousands of letters every day and had to meet strict performance measures with respect to answering them. The manager consistently beat the target year after year and was subsequently promoted. When the new boss met with his staff, he was taken aside and asked if he would be lenient on them if they told him the truth. After he agreed, they led him to a vault-like room in which he found hundreds of bags of unopened mail. Apparently the outgoing manager had ordered all mail to be bagged and stored in the room so that he could spend his days at home whilst still earning his promotion.

ANNOYANCE RATING

10 – No matter how crap work becomes, everyone seems to draw the line when it comes to the work-shy lazy bastards who draw a salary and deliver nothing in return. I reckon beggars put in more effort than the average Idle Git. At least they will carefully lay out their cardboard, cover themselves with a blanket and say "any loose change please." And they probably do longer hours, too.

RARITY

6 – Perhaps the Idle Git is a dying breed. Long gone are the days when you would regularly hear about people who would take their beds with them onto the night shift and sleep through to the morning with little or no redress. If management did raise an issue, the workers would go on strike. However, with regular recessions and jobs being transferred overseas, Idle Gits are gradually being transformed into Stress Junkies principally because they can't cope with even the lightest of workloads. Fortunately, doctors will sign anyone off with stress just to get them out of their surgeries.

SEASONAL VARIATIONS

The Idle Git will be more prevalent during the **summer months** when the opportunity to laze in the sun is too much of a pull. But then again, they are pretty widespread during the **winter** too, when they can use all manner of health-related excuses for not turning up to put in a full day's work. As you have probably noticed, the Idle Git is closely related to the Excuse Maker. After all, if you're going to be idle you'd better be good at making excuses.

AVOIDANCE|REVENGE STRATEGIES

1. Only work with industrious people who are prepared to put in a reasonable day's work and on whom you can depend.

2. Beware of anyone who claims they need more storage space than their fellow workers; it's only because they want to sleep in it.

3. Programme the tune "Lazy bones, sleeping in the sun, never get a days work done," into the Idle Git's mobile phone.

4. Ask them to spell work. When they spell it correctly, inform them that they have spelt it wrong and tell them in a loud voice it should be L-A-Z-Y-T-W-A-T.

5. Bring in a single bed and put it next to their desk, and why not throw in some maid service for good measure?

☐ Tick here when you have spotted the Idle Git

RATE THE
IDLE GIT'S
ANNOYANCE

The Jargon Junkie

GENERAL CHARACTERISTICS

The history and nature of the development of language throughout the world has fascinated anthropologists and linguists for centuries. Given that there are currently some 6,500 languages used regularly across the globe, it's no wonder we find foreign travel a daunting experience. But you would have expected that within the confines of the office, we would have developed a common language. Oh, how wrong can you be? There are those in our midst who insist on using a stream of incomprehensible words that appear to mean nothing at all. It's not language itself that's the problem, it's the use of jargon. The word "jargon" can be traced to the fourteenth century term for the twittering or warbling of birds. I prefer the modern definitions, which include the following: "an outlandish, technical language of a particular profession, group or trade," and "unintelligible writing or talk." I am sure that you have come across those people who you work with who use excessive amounts of jargon when normal words will do. Say Hi to the Jargon Junkie. The Jargon Junkie uses their jargon to:

- Feel part of a group.
- Deliberately confuse those around them.
- Show off – they may have nothing else to show off about, of course.
- Confuse and mislead.
- Make others feel stupid. Let's face it, how often do we challenge those that spurt such rubbish?
- Talk shite.

To be fair, most of us use jargon at some point in our careers, and it is an integral part of the daily grind. But when it is over the top, it just pisses people off. Some of the worst perpetrators are IT staff. They will use a stream of impenetrable language to convey even the simplest of messages. For example, in response to a basic statement, such as "my computer won't start, " they will typically reply with something like this: "Well, you see its your motherboard and if only you'd have rebooted whilst holding Alt Delete and then selected the run menu and pinged the mail server you would have been just fine." This use of techno-speak has been further extended by internet and text messaging, where practically every word has been truncated and all sorts of new ones invented. IMHO I TNK ITS BLX. I was told of one story which involved a perpetual Jargon Junkie and one of his staff. Instead of putting up with the continuous stream of inexplicable shite and the problems it created, this staff member decided to exact his revenge. Waiting until an important presentation, he prepared the slides for his boss but added a few extra twists which he embedded into the slideshow. Each time the presentation mentioned anything that was remotely jargon, the sound system would blare out "Danger, jargon alert". Unsure of how to respond, the Jargon Junkie continued. By the end of the presentation everyone was in stitches and the poor chap scurried out and was found some hours later in his office curled up in the foetal position. Some of the worst offenders are lawyers, solicitors and government officials. Nothing they say makes any sense at all, which may be the whole point, of course, because it means that no one feels able to challenge them. Another category of Jargon Junkie are those people who like to give themselves grandiose titles which somehow also give them the right to talk jargon. No longer can we call the guys who pick up our rubbish "Dustmen", we now have to call them "Sanitation Engineers". They don't travel in a dustcart anymore, it's a state of the art automatic excrement gathering receptacle. I fundamentally believe it is time to ditch jargon, so the next time you're faced by it, start to chant "What a load of bollocks" until the Jargon Junkie talks normally.

ANNOYANCE RATING

9 – Although the use of jargon may be annoying for those on the receiving end, it is unlikely to grate on those who belong to the group that use it. So although rated 9 on the annoyance scale, this is perhaps an external view. If you're in with the in crowd, the rating is likely to drop to 1.

RARITY

10 – Jargon Junkies are more common than guano in a penguin colony. Every function in every company has its fair share. From Finance to Human Resources, from IT to Marketing: they are all as bad as each other. All claim not to understand another group's jargon and yet vomit out a load of their own every time they open their mouths or put pen to paper. The Junkie is here to stay and may never die out.

SEASONAL VARIATIONS

None. People who insist on using jargon can't actually do much about it; it is hardwired into their brains (or what's left of them). After all, it is about belonging to a clique where you feel accepted. I guess that when people join an organisation they are almost jargon free, but over time they develop an unhealthy interest in the use of pointless words that mean nothing to the normal, but plenty to the deranged. In fact, if you took the trouble to ask them precisely what they meant, I am pretty sure they wouldn't know.

AVOIDANCE|REVENGE STRATEGIES

1. Talk in hieroglyphics, that way not even the Jargon Junkie can understand what the hell you are saying. Before long, you'll find yourself in a key technical position, like Chief Scientist or IT Director.

2. Point them in the direction of the Plain English Movement, designed to eliminate the excessive use of jargon.

3. Create a jargon detector and walk around the office identifying the excessive users of jargon.

4. Why not compile a jargon dictionary so that everyone can feel right at home no matter who they are talking to?

5. Develop a new form of jargon, involving the extensive use of profanities, and see how long it takes for it to catch on.

☐ Tick here when you have spotted the Jargon Junkie

RATE THE **JARGON JUNKIE'S** ANNOYANCE

The Leech

GENERAL CHARACTERISTICS

The recorded use of leeches in medicine dates back some 2,500 years to when they were used for bloodletting in Ancient Egypt. During medieval times a number of superstitions started to influence the practice of bloodletting and it wasn't long before leeches were being prescribed for all manner of complaints from mental illness to sexual deviancy. The use of leeches became so prevalent during the nineteenth century that the commercial leech trade became a major industry, with hundreds of millions of the bloodsucking mites in circulation, sucking the population dry. Returning to the modern day and the office environment, we can see that the leech is alive and well. The office-based Leech is someone who also sucks you dry, but not in a bloodletting sense. These are the individuals who are hungry for anything you might posses which they can steal and use for their own ends. They come in four major varieties, unlike the four hundred or so you find in nature:

- The Professional Leech. These are the people who will, as part of their career, leech as much as they can out of you. Typically they are people in credit agencies, lawyers, insurance salesmen, tax officials and so on. Although you might not work for them, you will certainly be stitched up by them.
- The Corporate Leech, often closely related to the Corrupt Bastard. The Corporate Leech will suck the very existence from the business either in terms of wasting money on stupid or pointless initiatives, paying themselves enormous sums of money for little return, or screwing up everything in sight. Having destroyed the business, they will get a handsome payoff and move on to the next company.

- The Knowledge Leech. These people will seek to extract as much of your knowledge as they can before you decide to leave the company. Such people offer crap training in return or, if you are particularly unlucky, no training at all. The result is that if you stay too long you are left brain-dead, with limited prospects. One organisation I was told about would bring bright young graduates in, bleed them dry and chuck them out. The company had a discipline of offering no training at all, apart from the usual health and safety stuff, which hardly added any value to anyone (apart from the Extracurriculars). People who worked there would gradually be dumbed down and many believed they would be better off becoming toilet attendants because they figured that offered better prospects.

- The Limelight Leech. These are those who will steal other people's ideas and pass them off as their own. They will ask you to produce a report, replace your name with their own and then offer it up to the boss to claim the fame and fortune that comes with it. Thomas Crapper is a good example. The man who claimed to have invented the flushing toilet was in fact a Limelight Leech. It was actually patented by a guy called Giblin. Mind you, telling someone that your going for a Gib doesn't have quite the same ring to it, does it?

One story involved an employee seeking revenge on his boss who would always pass off his subordinate's ideas as his own. So one day the guy wrote a paper about some new innovation and asked his boss to review it. Before long, it had reached the board and they were so excited that they decided to publicise it across the industry. Unfortunately for the boss, the paper had been plagiarised from another company's website and he got a severe drubbing from the directors.

ANNOYANCE RATING

7 – Unlike the leeches used in medicine, which appear to offer some kind of benefit, the office Leeches offer nothing whatsoever. They annoy us because the relationship is only one way; they seek to extract value from you and then use it for their own ends.

RARITY

6 – Most businesses can be considered to be leech-like, sucking as much as they can from employees. After all, that's the basis of most employment contracts. Equally there are plenty of Knowledge and Limelight Leeches who are out to enhance their careers by stealing the ideas and work from those around them. So the next time you come across a Nosey Parker, beware: they might just be a Leech in disguise.

SEASONAL VARIATIONS

Some Leeches, especially those that crave position and power, will do their best to claim credit for things **near appraisal time** in order to curry favour with their bosses. The majority will suck **all year round**. Perhaps if they are that good at sucking they should become prostitutes.

AVOIDANCE/REVENGE STRATEGIES

1. Try and work for people who will give you credit for the work you do.

2. Design a poster that warns staff about the Leech. Use a caption like "Leeches – they suck you dry".

3. Bring in a jar of leeches and pop a few into their coffee one morning.

4. Write a report that is patently wrong and allow the Leech to pass it off as their own (they will rarely read it). Once they get a kicking for it, they might just get the message that they are a bit of an arse.

5. Have Neighbourhood Leech Zones established around the office and promote someone to become a Leech officer whose job it is to patrol the floor looking out for Leeches (a great opportunity for the Extracurricular to add some value, for a change).

☐ Tick here when you have spotted the Leech

RATE THE **LEECH'S** ANNOYANCE

The Liar

E ach and every one of us lies. Some of the lies we tell are white lies, whilst others are huge porkies. Even a contest to find the world's biggest liar ended in allegations of cheating. The competition in which contestants are required to make up yarns in front of a panel of judges fell into disarray when the winner was accused of reading from a script and using props. Most lies go undetected to the untrained eye. But one of the things that really gets on workmates' nerves is the person who consistently lies. The Liar is someone who can't help but lie at every opportunity. These are the people who will say "I'll ring you back in five," or "You'll have the report on your desk first thing tomorrow morning." The reality is that they will not ring you back and they certainly won't have the report on your desk. Liars are closely related to Excuse Makers because they have to be able to back up their inability to deliver with a suitable excuse. The unfortunate thing about Liars is that they are everywhere and lying is endemic within the workplace. Many could lie for Britain. What's worse is that you end up bailing them out, because you or your colleagues care too much. The Liar comes in many different forms, the most common being:

- **The Executive Liar** who will spin you a yarn about how important you are to them and the company and how the promotion you have been looking for is just around the corner. Naturally the promotion doesn't materialise and you are given a whole raft of excuses as to why, with the carrot added that if you hang for a bit longer it will come. All they are doing is stringing you along and if you are so gullible as to accept this, then more fool you.

- **The Political Liar** *(see also the Politician)*. These people will play mind games with you in order to get their own way at your expense. The Political Liar will feign friendship whilst sticking a bowie knife between your shoulder blades. At least they will smile whilst are doing it.
- **The Deadline Liar.** Probably the worst kind of liar because they fool you into a false sense of security about their ability to deliver.
- **The Appraisal Liar** will concoct all manner of tales of achievement in order to bolster an otherwise lacklustre year.
- **The Compulsive Liar** who lies about everything.

The extreme version of the Liar is the Fantasist. The Fantasist is someone who lives on a different plane. They are not of this world and, because their life is so incredibly dull, will make up some fantastical lifestyle that they could neither afford, nor have the skill to pull off. This reminds me of the used car salesman in the film *True Lies* whose alter ego was a secret agent; in reality he was a lonely man who lived in a caravan park. Funny though this might sound, the fact is that there are millions of people out there who live their lives in some bizarre fantasy world. In fact, according to one survey, eight out of ten of us lie about what we do for a living. I remember meeting a guy once who purported to have hundreds of Rolex watches in his house. He also stated that he was Prince Charles's chef. Of course he was lying, as he lived on a run-down council estate and only wore a Swatch. Someone also told me of a college boy who was working in a warehouse. He told everyone around him that he wasn't really a warehouseman, he was a record producer and was in the process of putting a band together which would definitely result in a number one by Christmas. That Christmas came and went, as did many others.

ANNOYANCE RATING

5 – This varies according to type. Fantasists are quite harmless and if anything provide plenty of amusement for their colleagues. Their tales are so ridiculous you can't help but find them amusing and in any case they can become the butt of everyone's jokes. There are exceptions, though, as one fireman started blazes to impress his colleagues with his fire-fighting prowess. He's now in jail. The Liar who disrupts your deadlines, never comes back to you when they said they would, fails to deliver and generally lets you down is, of course, the most annoying kind.

RARITY

7 - It seems that more and more of us are lying. This is because most of us are out of our depth when it comes to work, blagging our way to positions we could never hope to hold down. There are also more of us who will lie about what we did at the weekend to make our lives appear far more glamorous than they actually are: "Oh, yeah, I went freefall parachuting this weekend." I don't think so, you were watching sport on the telly whilst eating chips in your underpants. Lying in this way is designed to demonstrate what great use was made of the weekend.

SEASONAL VARIATIONS

The Liar is more deadline-driven than most. They always sound incredibly keen at the beginning of a task only to let you down when it is too late for you to do anything about it. Mind you, some of these tactics are deliberate in some pains, such as the Politician. You will also find many more liars around **appraisal time**, when they will claim they have achieved much more than they actually have. And, boy, do we see many of these.

AVOIDANCE|REVENGE STRATEGIES

1. Only work with people you can trust (so, just yourself, then?).

2. Buy one of the many books that tell you how to detect Liars and leave it in a prominent position on your desk.

3. Carry a portable lie detector with you and subject them to random tests.

4. Outdo the Liar by claiming to be related to Tsar Nicolas II, saying that your great-grandmother survived the Communist firing squad by pretending to be a small rodent.

5. Suggest that they set up a website: Liars Reunited.

☐ Tick here when you have spotted the Liar

RATE THE
LIAR'S
ANNOYANCE

The Little Big Man

___

Some men find being short a very difficult thing to cope with. First, they tend to get stiff necks from having to look up at people when they talk to them. Second, women don't generally date men who are shorter than they are unless they are famous like Danny DeVito or Dudley Moore. Finally, their view is generally blocked by bigger people. It's no wonder, then, that some short chaps can end up with such huge chips on their shoulders. Some handle their height, or lack of it, very well and laugh at themselves when their colleagues come out with such tired witticisms as "there's no need to stand up… oh, you already are". Such a characteristic is always an endearing trait in anyone. But there are men out there who just can't cope with the fact they are a couple of feet nearer the ground than their colleagues and they over-compensate. Boy, do they over-compensate. Welcome to the Little Big Man. Little Big Men are people who are consciously aware of their stature and will do everything they can to compensate for it, including:

- Wearing built-up shoes.
- Using furniture that makes them look bigger.
- Driving sports cars because anyone looks good in them.
- Over-inflating their accomplishments.
- Only ever working with people who are shorter than they are, which in the main means children.
- Acting in an overbearing manner and intimidating staff, whilst standing on a crate.
- Marrying a midget.
- Becoming an infamous dictator like Adolf Hitler or Napoleon Bonaparte.

I'm afraid it matters to these people that they are little. It matters that they can only reach the groins of their colleagues. And it matters that everyone has to kneel on the floor when they want to speak to them. In extreme cases, the Little Big Man is so driven to make up for his limited size that he reaches for the sky. They will not rest until they have taken over the world and it should come as no surprise that a lot of Little Big Men run major corporations. Short people can get their revenge. One only has to look back into history to see that short men have dominated the world (in fact, most were both short and left-handed). Adolf Hitler was apparently a terrible guy to work for. He would interfere with all his generals' plans and would meddle in things he just didn't understand. And just imagine what a different world we would now live in had Adolf Hitler had been six foot six instead of five foot nothing. You see, the fundamental problem with Little Big Men is that they have to do everything they can to dominate those around them. Why? Because they can't dominate through height and many people don't take a short guy seriously. As a result some short men are driven and complete and utter bastards to work for; few are easy going. Things can get a lot worse when the Little Big Man has had no formal education. Not only are they vertically challenged, but they are intellectually challenged too (some might say they are close friends of the Village Idiot). I heard of one Little Big Man without any formal education at all who hated anyone who was smarter than he was. He would make himself look good by saying: "Do you know who I am? I am Giles who wrote the risk management framework for ABC corporation." Most people would just blank him and walk off.

ANNOYANCE RATING

6 – Compared to other pains in the office, the Little Big Man is perhaps not as irritating as some. However, there are instances when they can be especially annoying and that's when they start to behave in the same way as the career-obsessed Ball-Breaker. They over compensate for their lack of stature by being excessively political and competitive. Let's face it, it's the only way they can satisfy the need to become more important than anyone else. Exactly like the Ball-Breaker, their only target is the office of the CEO.

RARITY

5 – As the population continues to grow taller and wider, the number of Little Big Men is likely to reduce significantly. In medieval times, when diets were poor, the number of short people outnumbered anyone much above four foot three. These days, with improved diets, smaller people are increasingly looked down upon by tall people. In another fifty years from now there won't be any short people left at all.

SEASONAL VARIATIONS

None: the Little Big Man's behaviours don't really change at all with the seasons because he has stopped growing and his chips are now permanently attached to his shoulders. If you look

carefully, there is always this ray of optimism in their eyes that hopes that just like as nature, **spring** will somehow bring with it new opportunities for growth. Without drugs, this isn't going to happen.

AVOIDANCE|REVENGE STRATEGIES

1. Have a wooden crate or a set of stepladders handy so that the Little Big Man can get to your height when speaking to you.

2. Pose as a doctor and give them some suggestions on how to increase their height, from bone implants to using stilts.

3. Bring a saw to work and cut off the chips on their shoulders.

4. Put them on a rack and stretch them to normal height.

5. When they speak to you say "I'm sorry little boy, have you lost your mummy? Let me see if I can find her for you."

☐ Tick here when you have spotted the Little Big Man

RATE THE
LITTLE BIG MAN'S
ANNOYANCE

The Lovebirds

GENERAL CHARACTERISTICS

ex. Not much fun for one, better with two and amazing with three or more. But capping all is sex at work, because here you can combine sex with office furniture. Welcome to the Lovebirds. Long the preserve of the Alpha male, predatory sex is now all the rage with women too. According to the latest research, men now crave warmth and friendship, whilst women just want a damn good bonk. The combination of long hours, high-pressure jobs, the adrenalin that goes with it and the increasing numbers of women in the workplace are enticing more and more people into office affairs. Apparently, 46 per cent of unfaithful wives have had affairs at work, which compares quite favourably to the 62 per cent of men. Other surveys suggest that over 80 per cent of the working population have had some kind of sexual encounter at work. Married people often land affairs because it's the only place they face temptation and, watch out guys, you are more at risk from being snared by a sexually mature female than a nubile young office junior. Apparently 35 per cent of experienced women would have a casual fling. This is closely followed by the younger women, whilst older ones come in a poor third with few looking for an affair. Perhaps by then everyone has lost interest. Lovebirds come in many forms including:

- **The Party Poppers**, who will set off fireworks at the office party.
- **The Fantasy Flingers**, who love forbidden love.
- **The Photocopy F***ers** who will use all manner of office equipment to spice up their encounters.
- **The Toilet Seat Shaggers** who prefer privacy and the smell of dirty toilets and Domestos.
- **The Candid Cameras** who are caught on closed-circuit cameras and similar devices.

- The Lunchtime Lovers who will pop out to a seedy hotel for a quickie.
- The Genuine Daters who meet their future husband/wife at work. These are the most nauseating lovers you can hope to meet; no fun and far too treacly for their own good.

There are just too many stories of illicit affairs and one night stands to detail all of them, but here are a few:

- A man who worked for a training outfit was on a course when he needed to get some help from his boss. He searched high and low until he located him in a room nearby. As he broke the chair which was blocking the door he found his boss and an unknown woman busy at it. The boss's excuse was that he was trying to explain a particularly difficult training technique to her – probably something from the Kama Sutra.
- Some chap was at a post-merger training event with his company. As usual they retired to the bar following the training session to sink a few beers. As the night wore on they were joined by a woman from the other company. Now to describe this person as a witch was being kind. She had long black hair, black teeth and stained yellow hands from the cigarettes she chainsmoked. An hour or two later she was somewhat inebriated and fell over in the bar. A colleague picked her up and said that he would take her out for some fresh air. After another beer and another hour the rest of the group decided to turn in. The next morning they thought nothing of it until the trainer complained that he was tired because he had been kept awake by the noise from the couple next door who were screaming and grunting until sunrise. When quizzed on the matter the colleague came clean and admitted to shagging the witch.
- In the company where my wife used to work, a woman was caught on closed-circuit television having a quick one in the lift. I guess the guy involved must have had a hair-trigger problem because the building was only three storeys high.
- A woman who worked for a service company told me of the time when she was adjacent to a room in which the CFO of a client organisation was "taking" a woman from a rival company. Apparently he didn't stop and she squealed like a pig.

ANNOYANCE RATING

1 – I guess those who participate in an office fling, or indeed those who meet their future partners in the process, don't believe that they are annoying at all. What's more they can provide a wonderful source of gossip. The trouble comes when things don't work out and the affair ends. The fallout can be significant. Not only does it disrupt the people involved, but it usually affects their colleagues as well; some may have become involved in the web of lies designed to hide the affair, perhaps covered up for the all-too-regular absences. Bosses usually take a dim view as office affairs lead to reductions in productivity, but if it's the boss who's having the affair then it's usually considered to be an essential perk. In an attempt to buck the trend, some American companies are asking employees to sign "love contracts" to ensure that the parties concerned treat each other fairly when it all goes pear-shaped.

RARITY

10 – There is no doubt that office luvin' is on the rise. The increasing hours that people work, coupled with the intense pressure they find themselves under, means that there is little time for socialising. Throw in a healthy obsession with teamwork and you have all the ingredients for an affair. According to some, the increased divorce rate in the United States and Britain is the result of more and more people shedding their pants, knickers and bras in the workplace.

SEASONAL VARIATIONS

As always, **Christmas** will bring out more Lovebirds than usual. The combination of another tough year at work, plenty of booze and a conveniently located love shack a short lift ride away often proves too much of a temptation.

AVOIDANCE|REVENGE STRATEGIES

1. Keep whatever you have in your underwear firmly secured.

2. Always check the photocopier for telltale signs of buttock cheeks.

3. Install condom dispensers next to the coffee machine.

4. Send an anonymous note to the Lovebirds offering them a buy one, get one free offer for marriage guidance counselling.

5. Buy the Lovebirds a copy of *Dirty Little Secrets* – a book all about office affairs.

☐ Tick here when you have spotted the Lovebirds

RATE THE
LOVEBIRDS'
ANNOYANCE

The Martyr

GENERAL CHARACTERISTICS

In the past, and particularly during the religious turmoil of the sixteenth and seventeenth centuries, many men and women were prepared to die for their beliefs. Burning at the stake was not necessarily the best way to meet their Maker, but those who chose to be barbecued alive were satisfied that they had done the right thing by refusing to recant. I do hope they weren't disappointed; it would have been a real bummer to have died in vain. You would have thought that martyrdom had long since disappeared, but it is alive and well in the workplace. The Martyr is someone who loves to put themselves out for everyone around them. For them servitude is all that matters, which sets them aside from many other pains who are only willing to serve themselves, not least the Competitor, Politician and Career Bike. Martyrs are desperate to demonstrate their self-flagellatory capabilities in the hope that someone out there actually cares. If they think their peers or bosses really do, then they are seriously deluding themselves; I'm afraid the Martyr will be exploited until the pips squeak. Unlike many of their colleagues, the Martyr will work without complaint, and will undertake all manner of tasks, no matter how trivial or demeaning. I guess Martyrs wouldn't be quite so bad if they let up once in a while; took some time off and let off a bit of steam or something. Unfortunately they don't seem able to do so. They also love to come out with crazy statements like:

* "If you want something done, ask a busy person."
* "Don't worry about me, you run along and have a good time, I'll hold the fort."
* "I don't know why I stay here, but I suppose they just couldn't manage without me."

- "Sure, I'll come in at the weekend and finish that report; I've nothing better to do."
- "I haven't taken any holiday for the past five years... I don't believe I can justify it."
- "Sure, I will work all night. I was going to go the cinema, but I can cancel it."
- "I didn't have anything planned this weekend, so don't worry, I'll get that report finished."

You can imagine that as soon as they get home they start cleaning the house top to bottom or better still take on another job, like one at the Samaritans. I think one word sums up the Martyr: pathetic. Come to that, so is their sense of dress, which is always serf-like, plenty of dull colours and brown shoes. In fact, the best way to spot a Martyr is by their clothes. One Martyr I heard about did everything he could for the boss, the secretary, the receptionist, in fact anyone who would ask. The poor chap would work inhuman hours, do menial tasks (much to the amusement of his fellow workers), give up holidays when ordered to by his boss (which was pretty much every year) and yet did all this with the cheer of a Village Idiot. His martyrdom spilled out into his social life where his colleagues would get him to help them with their own domestic chores, like digging the garden, mending fences and even babysitting, whilst they put their feet up to watch sport on television or went out and got pissed with their mates. The guy was clearly exploited and was not the least bit worried about it. Unfortunately, his unending martyr-like deeds not only cost him his marriage (his wife, who was desperate to have children, never saw him and decided to have an affair) but eventually lost him his job too because, in a wave of work/life balance angst, the company accused him of being a workaholic and felt that his behaviour was setting the wrong example to staff. The problem with Martyrs is that they blithely allow themselves to be subjugated, exploited and brutalised by anyone who chooses to do it. In the end, I guess, they don't believe they have the right to object. Or perhaps it's because it has been preordained by their star sign.

ANNOYANCE RATING

3 – The Martyr is innocuous and not especially annoying. It's difficult to be upset by someone who wants to spend their working lives shovelling everyone else's crap. It used to pay very well in medieval times, but not so much now; I imagine that's because it doesn't smell quite so terrible.

RARITY

6 – There are a surprising number of Martyrs in offices. I think this must in part be due to the way most of us are treated by our employers and that so many people live in fear of losing their livelihood. Better to be subjugated than destitute. Mind you, I think there are quite a few employees who quite like being the Martyr and, if you believe their press, they are the people that hold most businesses together leaving the rest of us to play all the games we need to in order to get on.

SEASONAL VARIATIONS

Martyr-like tendencies tend to come out around religious ceremonies when they can make it evidently clear to all around them that they are true flagellants. Forsaking a good time for work is a clear sign of their conviction. Not quite the stake, but the next best thing. You will also see more Martyrs during the summer months when they will proclaim that they don't have the time for a holiday this year because everything will come crashing down without them. Get a life and take a holiday, you sad git.

AVOIDANCE|REVENGE STRATEGIES

1. Collect some wood with your colleagues, pile it up in the centre of the office and invite the Martyr to take their rightful place on the top of the pyre.

2. Ask them if that's the stigmata on their hands, or just red pen.

3. Offer them a hair shirt and a whip to lash themselves with.

4. Abuse them mercilessly. Give them all your shitty jobs and go down the pub.

5. Pose as Tomás de Torquemada. Order them to attend an Inquisition to test if they are a true martyr to their cause.

☐ Tick here when you have spotted the Martyr

*RATE THE
MARTYR'S
ANNOYANCE*

The Masticator

GENERAL CHARACTERISTICS

It is well known that if we don't chew our food properly it can lead to all sorts of problems, including choking and indigestion. Indeed, doctors recommend that we should chew each mouthful a minimum of thirty times to ensure the bolus is of sufficient size and consistency to aid absorption. I think we should adhere to such advice, but I also think it should be left out of the office environment, where discarded boluses can cause immense distress. The Masticator is, as you'd suspect, someone who eats their food in a way that causes disgust, horror and revulsion to their colleagues. The Masticator shares some of the Fast Fooder's (see *Pains on Trains*) annoying attributes including:

- Stinking the office out. Why do people insist on bringing all manner of pungent food to their desks? From curries to pasta replete with parmesan cheese, much of it smells of vomit and is the last thing you want to experience whilst attempting to complete that vital report for the boss. It is a form of olfactory abuse that should be stamped out.
- Leaving the mess about their own or, in most cases, other people's desks. It would be nice if they would clear up after themselves, but all too often you find your beautifully tailored shirt ruined by some animal who has left curry all over your desk. I have heard of extreme cases where people have left telephones covered in grease and computer terminals caked in bits of half-eaten and half-digested food.
- Poor manners. There is nothing quite so revolting as having someone sitting opposite you chewing their food with their mouth open or someone who talks with their mouth full. Before long you will find yourself either retching or covered in rice, curry, bread, cheese, soggy crisps or fruit.

Then there are the gum chewers who constantly grind their jaws, masticating, dribbling and speaking at the same time. It's quite remarkable that they can achieve so much simultaneously. The issue I have with this branch of the Masticator family is that, in the most part, they are morons who shouldn't be working in the first place. I also take umbrage at the way they discard their gum; usually on the underside of tables or on the edge of chairs. I am sure you, as well as I, have spent many a happy hour removing gum from your work clothes with a pair of tweezers. Of all the members of the Masticator family, the Gannet is probably the saddest. You will be able to spot them after any meeting that involves a buffet lunch. It is commonplace to over-order food for such meetings so that there is plenty left for those staff unfortunate enough not to be invited. While most will help themselves to one or two morsels as an unexpected bonus, the Gannet will make this opportunity their main source of sustenance. Their desk will typically be positioned so as to afford them a superb view of the meeting room; then, at one o'clock as the meeting adjourns, they pounce. Zooming in on the most precious delicacies, they will help themselves to as much grub as they can. Walking back, hands full and sandwiches hanging from their mouth, they are set up for the rest of the day. The Gannet is usually single and often male; they normally subsist on pot noodles, fast food, biscuits and crisps and for them this bonus is a treat. Research into the number of germs that exist in the office environment has highlighted a very interesting fact. Apparently, the amount of germs per square inch on the average office desk is 400 times greater than on the average toilet seat. So the next time you fancy having a meal at your desk, why not take it to the loo? What's more, if this is a hot curry you may as well stay put for it to come out the other end.

ANNOYANCE RATING

5 – The Masticator should not be allowed to eat in the office. The provision of local eateries and canteens are designed to give employees the opportunity to take a break and eat in a pleasant environment. In any case, eating on the fly isn't good for you.

RARITY

7 – Is it me, or is the number of Masticators rising? In these difficult times where we are all in danger of losing our jobs, the need to eat whilst working is a powerful force. We need to demonstrate to our bosses that we are totally committed to the firm and that we are willing to sacrifice our lunch hour to complete the impossible amount of work that has been set for us. But how can you be truly productive when you're stuffing your face with special fried rice? Just who are you trying to impress? Lets face it, whilst you are busy at your desk, your boss will be down the pub boozing it up.

SEASONAL VARIATIONS

The only thing that could change with the Masticator is the type of food they might eat. In general you should expect more curries, pasta meals and hot stinky concoctions during the **winter** months and more salads, fruit and seeds during the **summer**. So on this basis it is far better to be near the Masticator during the summer than the winter.

AVOIDANCE/REVENGE STRATEGIES

1. Wear a gas mask and place medical partitions around your desk.

2. Install a powerful extractor fan above the Masticator's desk.

3. Set up a fast food outlet offering all manner of smelly and bizarrely coloured food.

4. Stand over them with some Mr Muscle cleaner so that you can eliminate those nasty splodges and stains.

5. Cough over their food when they're not looking.

☐ Tick here when you have spotted the Masticator

RATE THE **MASTICATOR'S** ANNOYANCE

The Mental Masturbator

GENERAL CHARACTERISTICS

I f you are anything like myself, you enjoy the opportunity to discuss and debate the important issues facing your company. Indeed such discussions are critical if the business is to grow. At the same time, I also like people who are able to make a decision when it matters. They are able to weigh up all of the information before them and come to a suitable conclusion. Unfortunately, people with such skills remain in short supply in the typical office. You will see many more of what I call the Mental Masturbators. These are those who not only like the sound of their own voices (in the same way that the Great Bores of Today do) but are also incapable of making a decision outside of geological timescales. The Mental Masturbator is skilled in the art of delay and obfuscation. They will wax lyrical for hours on end about everything and nothing. The Mental Masturbator will:

- Talk continuously, usually in a monotone, about their subject. They pride themselves on being a brilliant exponent of verbal diarrhoea.
- Explore a topic exhaustively, looking at every angle and every conceivable option before reaching a conclusion – if at all.
- Derail any decision-making forum by stealing the floor and insisting on debating all of the issues at hand.
- Apply their masturbatory skills to the written word with equal fervour (see the Nitpicker).
- Won't actually say very much that makes sense, in the main.

Like their physical equivalent, the Mental Masturbator will work themselves into a lather until they reach their crescendo. They also have a tendency to foam at the mouth as their brain goes into overdrive and their ability to control their bodily fluids is lost in the excitement of the discussion. I was told of one government employee (although I am sure he is not the only one) who was king of the Mental Masturbators. He would hold meetings that would last for hours and hours. Nothing would be decided and he would spend ages talking about the ins and outs of a particular issue without ever arriving at a conclusion. In fact he would cover the same ground over and over again. People would sit there working out how much money was being wasted. Very often the meetings would drag on so long that people would gradually drift out of the room, making their excuses as they went. I also heard of one instance of a Mental Masturbator who worked in IT. Whenever he was presented with a task he would thrash it out in immense detail asking question after question. It often took longer for him to discuss the problem than it did for him to code it. Given that he was working in a project environment, his prevarication usually meant that the projects were delivered late. This went on for a number of years until there was an opportunity to sack him. Of course the Mental Masturbator can be a useful distraction for the Idle Git and others who prefer to do nothing during their working day. Here they can be used to waste the day talking and discussing topics which have no intrinsic value to the workplace but, because they take all day, also provide a fantastic opportunity for the workshy amongst us to avoid work. Naturally, Mental Masturbators will not realise they are being used for more sinister ends, but it can be a great way to pass your time. So if you are feeling lazy why not engage a Mental Masturbator about a particular topic on which they are considered an expert? If you combine it with a coffee or lunch you might even enjoy it (as long as they pay).

ANNOYANCE RATING

5 – How annoying the Mental Masturbator will be depends on where you work. If you find yourself working in an academic environment, or perhaps in government, mental masturbatory prowess will be well received and may well speed your promotion. Such organisations attract the Mental Masturbator because there is no requirement to deliver anything. If, however, you work in a fast-paced business, such as an investment bank, the Mental Masturbator will be exceptionally annoying and indeed is likely to be sacked because no one likes someone who takes more than a nanosecond to come to an obvious conclusion.

RARITY

5 – Again, this very much depends on where you work. As with annoyance, you would be hard pressed to find more than a handful of Mental Masturbators in a dynamic business, whilst in a less dynamic organisation they will be in plentiful supply.

SEASONAL VARIATIONS

You will find a few more Mental Masturbators in the **autumn** when the business schools chuck out the latest clutch of MBA graduates and rejects back into the workplace. For the next few months you will be surrounded by fervent advocates of mental masturbation. They will debate the importance of strategy, human resource management and many other topics that will, as always, fall on deaf ears. Rest assured, though, they will calm down when they realise that they actually have to do something for a living beyond talking bollocks.

AVOIDANCE|REVENGE STRATEGIES

1. Avoid those professions that attract Mental Masturbators.

2. Buy them books on effective conversation and decision making.

3. Pop a baby's dummy in the Mental Masturbator's mouth.

4. Offer them a box of tissues which they can use to wipe the foam from their faces on completion of their intellectual equivalent of a hand job.

5. Why not write a best selling book called *Mental Masturbation – Advanced Techniques*. In it you can describe the topics, techniques and attributes of the Mental Masturbator.

☐ Tick here when you have spotted the Mental Masturbator

RATE THE **MENTAL MASTURBATOR'S** ANNOYANCE

The Midas

The story of King Midas has fascinated people for thousands of years. The idea of some greedy old fart wanting more and more wealth and then getting his comeuppance is great. Despite the moral of the story – that greed is bad – it seems that there are those amongst the working population who believe the opposite is true. These are the people who just can't get enough. These are not the power-crazed Politicians we see at work but those obsessed with accumulating more and more wealth, be it in terms of hard cash, share options or payments into their pension pots. People like this are known as the Midas. Sure, we would all like to maximise our income; after all, otherwise why work? But it ought to be possible to draw the line when it comes amassing so much cash that you could never hope to spend it. What's worse is that those who do so never want to give up their job and do something more useful with their lives, like die, for instance. Though by the time they have decided it is time to hang up their boots with some massive fortune, it is highly likely they will expire shortly after retirement. Apparently if you retire after 65 your life expectancy is a paltry 18 months. If you retire at 55, you have something like 20 years left. But this sort of message is lost on the Midas. The Midas is usually attracted to certain types of jobs including:

- Sales, where they can make a fast buck by selling stuff you don't really want.
- Investment banking, where they can make a pile of cash by playing the markets.
- Insurance, where they can sell you investment and savings products that are just plain shite.
- Executive management, where they can line their pockets with vast sums of money whilst paying their staff next to nothing.
- Law, where they can fleece their clients for vast sums of money in legal fees.

If we look into the psychological theory of power and money we can see that as a Midas accumulates more and more wealth they become more and more concerned about losing it. Where on earth would they lose it? Out shopping? In the garden centre? Down the loo? So rather than stopping and taking time out to enjoy their lives (which is probably impossible), they continue to amass the cash. I guess it is about trying to show the world that they are a great success. The worst kind of Midas is the Executive Midas. They not only ensure that they are paid multimillion-pound salaries but then start complaining and bitching that they aren't paid enough. For Christ's sake, give it a rest. One senior banker even went on record to say that his £2 million plus salary was not enough and that, compared to others in his sector, he was poorly paid. Poor baby, mummy will make it better for you. Maybe you could get the staff to give you a whip round. Even the bloody Simpsons have been at it. The actors who provide the voices were no longer satisfied with the paltry $125,000 per episode they were getting for their work (this involves talking for a maximum of 30 minutes); they wanted $360,000 and threatened to strike. They got their way – Homer, what a greedy little Midas you are. What's worse is when a Midas asks you to guess how much they earn or insists on telling you how rich they are. I heard a story of this jumped-up worm of a man who insisted on asking his subordinates to guess how much he was paid. Most, as you would expect, declined but this didn't stop him from revealing that he brought home near seven figures. This chap has a lot of friends, of course. Other tactics employed by the Executive Midas include awarding themselves pay rises when the company is going to the wall, cutting headcount and staff salaries whilst lining their own pockets and harping on that they have to be paid vast sums of money to keep up with the market. Yes, that must be the market that is determined by all their friends on the remuneration committee, who are paid enough to keep their mouths shut and comply with the needs of the chief executive's cocaine habit and obsession with Eastern European prostitutes. When a Midas gets out of control there is a real danger that they might become a Corrupt Bastard, whose craving for cash knows no bounds.

ANNOYANCE RATING

10 – The Midas scores a bullseye, but not because they earn so much and are sad enough to keep working when they could give up at any time. It's because they abuse their positions by pushing up their salaries higher and higher and then complaining that they still don't get enough. Such winging is not only pathetic and smacks of a spoilt brat not getting his or her way, but is also badly received by staff who view their senior executives as a bunch of arseholes who are only there to line their own pockets.

RARITY

5 – The US influence on the boardroom has resulted in a stampede of Midas-like behaviour with every board member grabbing as much money, options and pension contributions as they possibly can. Celebrity CEOs are famous for it, spending lavishly on their homes, their families and themselves. Private jets, extortionately expensive shower curtains, even gold leaf bog roll. The key question we should all ask ourselves is would we do the same? If, as I suspect, the answer is yes, then we must all be latent Midases waiting patiently for our turn.

SEASONAL VARIATIONS

Midases will seek to maximise their income **all year round**. The Executive Midas will usually start bitching around the end of year when reporting annual results to the city and complaining that they aren't getting paid enough.

AVOIDANCE/REVENGE STRATEGIES

1. Work for a charity. It may be full of weirdos, but at least you won't come across any Midases.

2. Dip your fingers into some gold paint so that everything you touch turns to gold.

3. Dress up as an nineteenth century gold prospector and shout "There's gold in them thar boardrooms".

4. Draw a simple chart that indicates the disparity in pay between the board and the employees and use this to incite rebellion.

5. Envy mark their Mercedes and slash its tyres.

☐ Tick here when you have spotted the Midas

RATE THE **MIDAS'S** ANNOYANCE

The Mismanager

GENERAL CHARACTERISTICS

The day you started your first job was probably the first day you aspired to become a manager. Not satisfied with having a role that entailed creating or delivering something, all you wanted was that elusive title and ability to boss other people around. I used to laugh with my colleagues about who would end up running the business we had all joined. Although we all wanted it, none of us made it; in any case, none of us work there any more, so I guess it's all a bit academic. Management has vexed both academics and practitioners alike for millennia, mainly because a manager doesn't actually do anything. Knowing this, why on earth does someone want to become a manager? Maybe it's the title or the power. Or perhaps it just about getting more cash and having the authority to beat people up. Whatever it is, the unfortunate thing is that there are many managers out there who have reached their level of incompetence. They are living examples of the Peter Principle (being promoted to their level of incompetence). Such people are known as Mismanagers. Mismanagers are, in essence, crap at their jobs; they are everything a manager should not be. They couldn't even manage their way out of a paper bag without upsetting the bag. The Mismanager comes in a number of different guises, including:

- **The Seagull**, who flies into your function, team or office, dumps all over you and then flies out again leaving you to wonder what the hell that was all about.
- **The Mushroom**, who will try and keep you in the dark and every now and then cover you in manure. This type of Mismanager is particularly prevalent during reorganisations when they will claim to know nothing about what's going on even though they are among the architects behind it.

- **The Kipper**. Like their fishy equivalents, these people are two-faced and have no guts. This type of Mismanager is one of the worst as you really can't trust them to do anything. Having said that, you can spot them a mile off because they stink of fish.
- **The Meeting Muppet**, who insists on having a meeting about anything and everything. This ensures that their diaries are filled with fruitless get-togethers which typically achieve nothing, thereby preventing them from doing any real work.
- **The Buck Passer**, who rather than take the responsibility for a decision likes to pass the onerous duty onto someone else.
- **The Monkey**, who will always come out with statements like "I hope you're not going to leave the monkey on my shoulder" whenever you ask them for help. As with all Mismanagers, this absolves them of all responsibility. The Monkey will see themselves as a facilitator rather than a doer.
- **The Nice But Ineffective.** Although a generally nice individual whom you could quite happily stay in the pub with all afternoon, the NBI is usually totally useless at getting anything done, looking after staff or indeed anything apart from buying you a pint.
- **The Joker**, who loves to be one of the lads and would rather be messing about and joking than working. To them it's all a game show and they are the host.
- **The Mute**, who does not believe in any oral communication at all and instead will resort to email or tiny pieces of paper.

The Mismanager is often combined with other pains, including the Egotist and the Bully, which does not bode well for their staff. I heard of one Mismanager who was of the Mute variety and had bullying tendencies. As a project manager he had to sit with his staff. But instead of talking to his team directly, he would send them emails and put labels and pieces of paper with handwritten messages on their desks. He would even have ones that read "can I have a word, please?" which was terribly ironic as he had the communication skills of a koala bear. Most of his staff applied the volcano principle to his notes; once any of the innumerable slips of paper fell onto the floor they would assume they were no longer relevant and would claim that they had not seen the original message.

ANNOYANCE RATING
10 – The Mismanager is another pain who scores ten out of ten, mainly because they are the ones who destroy so much value in the places we work. However, they are the butt of most people's jokes and quips about work, so perhaps 10 is too high. I will let you be the judge of that.

RARITY
7 – With so few people doing a real job these days, we have seen the ranks of Mismanagers swell beyond reason. They are absolutely everywhere, each and every one of them suitably unqualified to do the jobs they have. Soon there will be no one actually working for a living.

SEASONAL VARIATIONS
Mismanagers will be with us **all year round**, along with their incompetence.

AVOIDANCE/REVENGE STRATEGIES
1. Work for a decent manager.

2. Attempt to improve their management skills by buying them a subscription to a number of management magazines, such as the *Harvard Business Review* – though this may run the risk of transforming them into a Jargon Junkie instead.

3. Suggest they star in a Boss Swap programme on television to highlight just how crap they are.

4. Give them a copy of the script of *The Office* so that they can improve their crap management skills or at least make them funny.

5. Buy them a tie with a W and a picture of an anchor beneath it.

☐ Tick here when you have spotted the Mismanager

RATE THE
MISMANAGER'S
ANNOYANCE

The Moaner

GENERAL CHARACTERISTICS

Some people are just never satisfied. Whatever they have, it is never enough. You see this with celebrities obsessed with buying all manner of pointless trinkets and you see this at work with those who always want more. Whether it's money, status, power, staff or paperclips, their needs will never be sated. And, boy, do they want to tell you about it. Welcome to the Moaner. Moaners will see their working lives as a succession of setbacks and failures, none of which are their fault, of course. Their misfortune is always down to other people who have got it in for them or extenuating circumstances that have confounded their well-laid plans. It was their boss, their staff, the fact that they are an Aries: never that they are rubbish or have reached their natural ceiling. They are workplace victims and what's worse is that they are likely to tell this to anyone who'll listen. But they don't stop there, oh no. They also love to enlighten you about the other miseries in their lives, from their pathetic relations and unruly children to the state of the nation and the fact that we would all be better off dead. They are the mood hoovers in the office, sucking all the joy and fun out of an environment that is seriously deficient of fun in the first place. There are a few different types of Moaner whom you should avoid at all costs:

- **The Past Over and Pissed Off.** These are the people who will never make it to the top and have not quite realised that the aspirations which they had when young will never be realised. They are passed over for promotion year after year and are soooo stupid that they have yet to recognise that they are well and truly on the scrapheap. Even when they are told that they will never get that elusive promotion into middle management, they still harbour dark desires for power.

- **The I Deserve Better Than This.** These are the employees who believe that they are worth more than they are getting, be it in terms of hard cash or status. They will come out with statements such as "I'm 43 and I'm still only a photocopier clerk," and expect you to show some sympathy. Perhaps "Can you do me a hundred copies of this, please?" might be a suitable retort.
- **The Rainman.** No, this has nothing to do with a film about an autistic man and his exploitative brother; it has everything to do with the people who walk around the office with a constant rain cloud above their heads. These people move about the building with furrowed brows and a morbid sense of purpose. For them it is about getting through another pointless day in the office. They are the modern day equivalents of Atlas, holding the whole business on their shoulders. No time for small talk and no time for fun. Just work, work, work…
- **The Sabre Rattler.** These people are your colleagues who are constantly threatening to leave, saying how awful their jobs are and how it's about time they left for pastures new. The first time they say this you might think "good for them", but when they have been making the same statement year after year it gets a tad boring. If you are going to leave don't talk about it, take a leaf out of Nike's book and "just do it".
- **The Auto Grumbler.** These are the people who are professional grumblers. No matter how good it gets, you can guarantee they will find something to moan about. Even when they have the plushest office, the largest salary and best perks, they will continue to complain.

I heard about one Moaner who would state every January how shite work was and that he was going to get another job. Years passed by and still no action. Then someone decided to help him out. They found this ideal position for him using all his skills, cut out the advertisement and showed him. He showed mild interest so someone offered to rewrite his CV to suit the role. Everyone waited, waited and waited. Nothing happened and even though the Moaner was offered a plumb opportunity to get off his backside and do something, he did nothing. In fact he is still with the same employer, and no doubt still complaining.

ANNOYANCE RATING

8 – Sure, we all have bad days at work and it often seems like we are wasting our lives turning up to the same employer year after year, but then we have little choice as we need to keep ourselves from sleeping rough and smelling of urine. The problem with Moaners is that they don't stop; their moaning is incessant. And no one, not even the Pope, could cope with that.

RARITY

6 – Despite the drive to make work fun and exciting there are many, many Moaners out there. Their numbers have swelled as employers have cut back perks and generally treated staff with contempt. That said, there is always a case for put up or shut up.

SEASONAL VARIATIONS

You will see many more Moaners during the **annual appraisal period**, when they will always have plenty to complain about. The level of grousing increases dramatically when they find that their pay rise this year is two-fifths of f**k all and they have been overlooked for promotion again. Hardcore Moaners will hang on but the momentarily disgruntled will up sticks and move on. If zero pay rises continue for too long you will soon find yourself surrounded by more Moaners than you can shake a stick at.

AVOIDANCE|REVENGE STRATEGIES

1. Organise a sponsored moanathon.

2. Only work with happy people, but be careful not to hang out with the Tree-Hugger.

3. Buy them a clown outfit complete with thick red theatrical paint for their happy face.

4. Buy them a voodoo doll so that they can use its magical powers to exact their revenge on their boss, their wife, kids, the Prime Minister...

5. Give them the number of a therapist who will be able to explore why they moan so much. This will probably surface deep-seated problems with their parents, the local vicar and even their rabbit, who bit them on the nose when they were six.

☐ Tick here when you have spotted the Moaner

RATE THE
MOANER'S
ANNOYANCE

The Nitpicker

GENERAL CHARACTERISTICS

You have spent hours on the report, poured over it to make sure it is suitably crafted, coherent, consistent, complete, clear, concise and factually correct. All in all, a fine job. You then hand it over to your boss. A few hours later it is dumped on your desk covered in red ink. How do you feel? Well, pretty pissed off, I should think. Welcome to the Nitpicker. This is the pain who, no matter what you do, will pick holes in it. So whether it is a presentation, an important project, an advertising campaign, a press release or pictures of your kids, they will find something wrong. You see, the Nitpicker does not care about what you think, they are far more concerned about getting their point of view across and making you look like a complete and utter moron. The Nitpicker comes in four main forms:

- **The Red-Penned Prat,** who will smother your work in red ink in the same way that your teachers did at school. There is nothing quite as satisfying as returning a report covered in red ink; it's payback time for all those years at school when there was no opportunity to fight back. Most people love to have the power of the red pen, but to have the pen that controls all other pens is a force of immense evil and one that is coveted by all office workers. I can see a book in this, maybe a blockbuster film, perhaps I should call it *The Fellowship of the Pen*.
- **The Grammar Geek**, who loves to pick you up on any grammatical mistake irrespective of whether it is written or spoken. The Grammar Geek is also someone who is obsessed with language, punctuation and grammar. Sure, the inappropriate use of the English language is annoying, but the Grammar Geek takes it to the extreme, even writing books about it. Pedants rejoice – bestselling books, which everyone buys, but only sad gits use. Grammar goes the same way as the Atkins Diet. In fact we'll be eating it next; a national

fixation for vacuous people. Not content with picking holes in your written words, the Grammar Geek will do the same with the spoken word. They will correct you at every opportunity with comments like "No, no, I think you meant coarse, not course," or "I think the word you should have said then was antidisestablishmentarianism, not bollocks."

- **The Revisionist**, who will keep on asking you to revise your work, over and over and over again. Each time you get the "Have you got a minute?" you know that you'll have your work cut out. They will lay out the new changes as well as the changes on changes they want you to make. They are masters of prevarication and indecision, but what is so intensely irritating about all this is that you know that on the tenth revision your work will be where it was when you first completed it.

- **The Invisible Jigsaw Puzzler.** These people are a particularly virulent form of Nitpicker who will never tell you what they actually want or need from you, leaving you to play the invisible jigsaw puzzle game. This involves you trying to second-guess what they want and then getting beaten up for not delivering it. Eventually you might get there, but it is a painful and pointless journey.

I heard of one poor guy who had to suffer one Nitpicker for three whole years. The reports and projects this chap worked on didn't last a few days, they ran into weeks and very often months. The Nitpicker would set a task and on being presented with the final report or the project's results would rip it apart and accuse the poor guy of not delivering what he wanted. Not only would the report come back smothered in red ink, but it would be covered in Tippex, Post-its and pieces of paper stapled over the original. Little was salvageable. Then, when the poor sod had completely rewritten it, the Nitpicker would do the same thing again. Finally, oh rapture: the Nitpicker was caught out. The victim was set a task by the Nitpicker in the presence of another manager and when he returned, having diligently completed the task, the Nitpicker (true to form) stated that he had failed to deliver to specification. Then, from the other manager, came: "Oh yes he has, Henry." The Nitpicker turned bright red and from that moment on behaved himself. I have heard of other Nitpickers who have forced people to rewrite reports over the weekend or to other ridiculous deadlines. In some instances this has induced heart attacks in their victims.

ANNOYANCE RATING

10 – The Nitpicker drives everyone mad. Why can't they just delegate the job and let you get on with it? Is it that they wish they were writing it, don't they trust you, or is it that they feel this is the only way they can add value? Some or all of these are true. You also have to wonder if they have nothing better to do. Of course they usually think they are adding value but in reality all they do is suck value and fun out of the business with their pedantic obsessions.

RARITY

8 – Nitpicking is a profession in its own right, and there are plenty of people around the office who believe it is their god-given right to pull other people's work apart. Nitpicking is both popular and common.

SEASONAL VARIATIONS

None. The Nitpicker's behaviours seem to be driven by the clock rather than the sun. They love the chance to unravel even the best work through their flamboyant use of their red pen especially when up against tight deadlines.

AVOIDANCE|REVENGE STRATEGIES

1. Pose as Hughie Green and say to them "It's make your mind up time".

2. If working to a deadline (ideally an external one) leave the final review to the last minute so that the Nitpicker has no time to get out the red pen.

3. Ask them why they don't become a teacher, or better still a school inspector.

4. Buy a copy of *Eats, Shoots and Leaves* and surgically implant it in their anus.

5. Find something they have written, pass it off as your own, and when it's torn to pieces, confront them in the style of Roger Cook or a similar investigative journalist.

☐ Tick here when you have spotted the Nitpicker

RATE THE
NITPIACKER'S
ANNOYANCE

The Nosey Parker

We have already been introduced to the Gossip, who is someone you might choose to use as part of your armoury to get on in the workplace, or choose to avoid if you don't fancy becoming a laughing stock. Let me now introduce you to the Nosey Parker. Nosey Parkers are subtly different from Gossips, in so far as they need to know about everything, not just the juicy snippets of information about what people are getting up to. In fact, for the most part they don't really care about digging up the dirt, as all they want to do is to find out as much about you and what you are up to as possible, which is terribly disconcerting. Don't get me wrong, because I think it is vitally important that each and every one of us maintains a grasp on what's going on around us, and in order to establish healthy relationships at work it is necessary to get to know a little about your colleagues. The trouble is that the Nosey Parker goes too far. Not satisfied with knowing your name, they want to find out about:

- Your extended family, their relationships, ailments, where they live and what they do.
- Where you are going on holiday, how much it costs, which airline you are travelling with and so on.
- Where you live, what your partner does, where your kids go to school, what their favourite subjects are and who their friends are.
- What you plan to do with your life both inside and outside of work.
- How you intend to be buried and what sort of service you'd like to have.

Why on earth do they want to know so much about you? Is it because they want to steal your identity? Is it because they are budding detectives who are desperate to practise and hone their skills? Or maybe it's because they are military interrogators, hunting down international terrorists? No, it's because they are interfering gits, who have nothing better to do than stick their noses into other people's business. Not satisfied with trying to find out everything there is to know about your life outside work, they will pry into what's happening inside the office too. They will interrupt your discussions to ask what you are talking about and force you to recap what has been said so far. Throughout the day, they will constantly pester you to find out what you are up to. You see, the Nosey Parker is someone who hates being on the sidelines. They want to be involved and engaged with what you and other people are doing. The Majority of Nosey Parkers are women for the simple reason that their brains are wired differently than men's; most men will talk about three subjects – work, sport and sex – but women will talk about everything under the sun. Men tend only to be interested in the competitive aspects of their colleagues so that they can ascertain whether they are a threat or not. Women will talk to anyone. I heard of one Nosey Parker who would spend the majority of her day asking people about themselves. From finding out about their childhoods to asking them what their favourite colours were, it didn't stop. This went on for some time until the lunchtime one of her colleagues was rooting through her desk drawers to find a document when she happened to find a stack of diaries. Each one contained incredibly detailed descriptions of the people she had been quizzing around the office. They included what they wore on a particular day, what they had for lunch, what their kids did at school, in fact pretty much everything. When she came back from lunch she was hauled in to see her boss. After a long discussion, plenty of tears and the occasional raised voice, it transpired that she was doing it as part of her research for a novel about work. Apparently, she had always wanted to write a book and thought this was great way to capture the material. Unfortunately for her, no one else did and she had to throw them away.

ANNOYANCE RATING

6 – How much the Nosey Parker annoys you will depend on the type of person you are. If you are an introvert like me, who doesn't really want some fool asking probing questions all the time, then quite a lot. However, if you are one of the many extroverts around the office, then you'll probably love it and will almost certainly ask just as many questions as they do. Also, if you happen to be an Idle Git, you will love them too because they give you a fantastic opportunity to do nothing but chat all day. However, the truly annoying aspect of the Nosey Parker's behaviour has to be the way they feel compelled to stick their beak into your business.

RARITY

3 – Thankfully there are comparatively few Nosey Parkers in the office. As work has become more inhuman and as people have become more unfriendly towards each other, the ranks of Nosey Parkers have diminished significantly. I guess this is because everyone is too busy trying to avoid the sack.

SEASONAL VARIATIONS

The Nosey Parker's behaviours will ebb and flow with the various comings and goings of the other staff in the office. In particular, they love to attach themselves to the new joiners, who offer a new target for their non-stop probing. You will also see more of them during **appraisal time**, as they will be desperate to find out what grades people have got, what salary increases they have secured and who is up for promotion.

AVOIDANCE|REVENGE STRATEGIES

1. Perform a tonguectomy so they can't ask you any more mindless questions.

2. Install microscopic cameras about their desk to capture what they are doing.

3. Give them dark glasses so they can be more subtle.

4. Offer to write their memoirs and call this The Night of the Long Nose.

5. Place a freshly laid turd on their desk and then ask them to stick their nose into your business.

☐ Tick here when you have spotted the Nosey Parker

RATE THE
NOSEY PARKER'S
ANNOYANCE

The Political Corrector

The world has indeed gone mad. Whatever we do and whatever we say we increasingly have to guard against the communal tyranny known as Political Correctness. Political Correctness began in the 1980s when a few bureaucrats took umbrage at those people in society who would transgress the norms of behaviour and offend other members of their community by their use of inappropriate language. Before long people were finding themselves hauled through the courts having to defend themselves for actions which had hitherto seemed quite innocuous. And shortly after that companies started to talk about diversity in order to avoid lawsuits for discrimination. These days you can be taken to an industrial tribunal by homosexuals, women, transsexuals, men, short people, old people, young people, smelly people, hairy people, obese people, puppies, gerbils and the occasional fox. In fact political correctness has got out so of hand that you could probably be sued for almost anything. It is clear that by saying anything that is remotely risqué you can risk being attacked in the street, taken to court, losing your job and in extreme cases receiving death threats. You're better off sewing your mouth up. We see the outcomes of the Political Corrector's actions all too often:

* A recent story involved a prison officer who made some remark connecting Bin Laden, Muslims and terrorists. This remark was picked up by the governor who sacked the official for racism. During the industrial tribunal it was revealed that the governor was so obsessed about political correctness that he would interpret anything out of the ordinary as being offensive.

- Quangos set up to ensure that government officials are not upsetting anyone. One case involved a councillor being investigated after becoming involved in a dispute about a mobile phone mast. His use of a loud hailer inflamed the local school so much that they felt he was acting unethically, leading to the allegations of sleaze.
- Another man was scrutinised after he refused to eat a local woman's bread in communion.
- Kilroy-Silk, who was sacked from his TV talk show because of remarks he made in the press about Arabs.

Let's face it, Political Correctors can use any excuse they like to get what they want or, indeed, to avoid work: "I can't work because I am a one-legged dwarf on crack." In this respect they have a lot in common with the Idle Gits but are less subtle about it. Political Correctors also suck any joy out of work because they eliminate any opportunity for laughter, spontaneity or genuine fun. I believe that it has been the unhealthy focus on political correctness that has led to a rise in the number of Tree-Huggers – those people who try to instil a false sense of jollity into the office, so long as it is politically correct. Things have become so bad that some experts have started to issue guidelines about office humour. One such guideline suggested that humour should be restricted to those acts that involve some kind of surprise or exaggeration that makes people feel good. The author of said advice then goes on to recommend leaving a biscuit on a colleague's desk as that would be considered acceptable because it conveys a sense of unity or support. What a complete load of bollocks. If someone left a biscuit on my desk I would be deeply concerned about their mental wellbeing (but I'd eat the biscuit first). The only people who would find this amusing would be those who have no sense of humour at all. Let's face it, most of the fun at work is derived from other people's misfortune and snuffing this out is a bit of a drag. All we can hope for is a backlash, which might be a long wait. Political Correctness is a bit like Prohibition, plenty of people policing ridiculous policies who swear and behave in the most appalling ways in private. I guess you can do what you want outside of the office, as there no one gives a tinker's cuss.

ANNOYANCE RATING

8 – The Political Corrector causes a significant amount of angst because of the need to guard against what you say. The problem is that the Political Corrector and, indeed, political correctness in general is an affront to the freedom of speech, which after all is designed to act as a check against extremism. Some organisations are akin to living in Stalinist Russia, where if you complained about food shortages that were not officially recognised you became an enemy of the state and if you failed to praise an old hero you would find yourself jailed, tortured and sent off to the salt mines. Although the punishment is not quite as severe, the conditions under which we have to work are just as harsh.

RARITY

10 – There is no doubt the Political Corrector is ubiquitous. Naturally you will see more in some offices than others. A typical investment bank will have comparatively few and indeed be dominated by schoolboy and toilet humour, but a government department, local council or anything that involves public services will be full of them.

SEASONAL VARIATIONS

The depressing thing about Political Correctors is that they will be with you, full on, **all year round**. Their obsession with what people say or write is a full-time occupation which rarely varies throughout the year. Mind you, **Christmas** is a good time to see them in action, making sure there are no offensive statements about dwarfs, overworked reindeer or comments about bearded old men in red suits. In fact, the Political Corrector would like to rewrite the whole story with vertically challenged helpers, Person Christmas who is bound to be an asexual, multiracial, temporarily employed person with a group of organically raised, well-adjusted reindeer.

AVOIDANCE|REVENGE STRATEGIES

1. Never offend anyone at work... save it for the pub.

2. Issue the Political Corrector with a copy of 1984, which should give them plenty of ideas.

3. Develop a new rule book for the office, which will only allow staff to discuss flowers and fruit and then only in designated areas.

4. Place signs around the office informing staff of all the things that are banned, you know: laughter, smiling, fun, etc.

5. Make as many politically incorrect statements as you can. When the inevitable investigation follows claim your right to free speech under the Human Rights Act.

☐ Tick here when you have spotted the Political Corrector

RATE THE
**POLITICAL
CORRECTOR'S**
ANNOYANCE

The Politician

Aristotle was right, Machiavelli was an arch-practitioner, John Major a mere amateur. All of us have to embrace it; few of us want to. Yes, politics, that dark force within all organisations. Although work-based politics is not quite as extreme as that played out between members of political parties, who will shaft each other at every opportunity, nor perhaps as deadly as the medieval court, where you could literally lose your head if you stepped out of line, it is just as significant. You ignore it at your peril. Those who take up its siren call play a dangerous game which can lead to greatness or the wilderness. The Politician is someone who plays politics for a variety of reasons including:

- They want power.
- They want more power.
- They want even more power than that.
- They want absolute power.
- But they also want revenge (power again), to ruin other peoples careers (yep, you've guessed it: power) or to become a real politician (plain stupidity).

As in politics with a big P, Politicians are people you cannot trust, because no matter how sincere they appear, they only have one thing on their mind – themselves. Never kid yourself that they have your interests at heart, especially when they say such things as "I'm with you, shoulder to shoulder," because at the first sign of trouble you'll find yourself standing next to the invisible man. The Politician is the master of linguistic fog and a heavy user of spin. They will spin their words in whatever way they can to reflect a view that can

be interpreted in any way by any person. They are always indirect and love to turn your question to them into a question for you. So, never expect an answer that doesn't start with "it depends" or "what do you think?" Politics is a bit like masturbation. A lot of people claim to avoid it because it is dirty, immoral and makes you go blind. But in private they toy with it furiously, watching in wonderment at the mess it makes. As you might suspect, the Politician is a very close cousin of the Egotist and the Corrupt Bastard, although far more subtle. Many people have told me stories of Politicians and how they became beguiled by their velvet tongues. One story involved a guy who worked in IT. He loved his job and was apolitical. He had been tipped for promotion to IT Director and assumed, quite naively, that it was a done deal. He confided in a fellow senior IT guy about his aspirations and the great ideas he had for the IT Department once he was in post. Unfortunately for him, the chap he confided in took his ideas, wrote a paper to the CEO and – hey presto – was instantly promoted to IT Director. The hapless colleague complained (bad idea) to the CEO who thought he was being childish. You see, the Politician cares little for those who get in their way and those who complain just look like spoilt brats crying to mummy. Furthermore, the other thing that sets Politicians aside from the nice people at work (and just who are they, I wonder?) is that they have such thick skin that nothing gets to them. They have had any emotions surgically removed. They are the embodiment of the survival of the fittest.

ANNOYANCE RATING

6 – The problem with the Politician is that you rarely know you've been shafted until after the event. The expert Politician is a master at the sleight of hand. You will be drawn into their confidence and used and abused as they see fit. Then, when no longer required, you will be dropped like a hot potato, reputation sullied and career in tatters. I often hear of people who believe what they are told only to be shat upon later and yet, when they are told about it they suddenly see the light, only to repeat the same mistakes time and time again. I guess such people are just gullible or just plain stupid.

RARITY

9 – In these politically charged times everyone needs to be a Politician in order to tread the fine line between becoming a hero or zero. But beware the amateur who is so utterly transparent that they might as well wear a T-shirt that says "I'm trying to be political, but I am really crap". These are the idiots who can't hold their tongues and will let slip their plans to others without checking out who they might be aligned to. It isn't long before they find themselves unable to sit down from the severe rogering they get as a consequence of their friend blabbing to other people.

SEASONAL VARIATIONS

The Politician is particularly conspicuous during the run-up to **major promotion rounds**. Those in the running will spend their time wining and dining the people in power, discrediting the other contenders and attempting to demonstrate their leadership skills with staff. When there is a significant six figure income involved, they will unleash all of their slimy skills and capabilities in order to get what they desperately want. And what they really, really want is power, the Lear Jet, the multimillion-pound lifestyle and all the Company Bikes they can ride.

AVOIDANCE|REVENGE STRATEGIES

1. Embrace politics. If you don't, you deserve everything you get.

2. Only work with people who talk straight; you know, the person who will say "I call a spade a spade, me, and if you don't like it you can get out". The trouble is that they can be a real pain in the arse too (so not a great solution).

3. Bring a plastic baby into work and give it to the Politician; they'll love this.

4. Give them a copy of the Ojays' single *The Backstabber*.

5. Write their biography and call it *The Life of a Scheming Bastard*.

☐ Tick here when you have spotted the Politician

RATE THE **POLITICIAN'S** ANNOYANCE

The Road Block

GENERAL CHARACTERISTICS

Change is an integral part of office life. In fact, no sooner has the company been reorganised then the next grand initiative is launched in a hail of enthusiasm from management and received with the usual cynicism from staff. Everyone ends up going through the motions, knowing that nothing will actually change and that they can largely stay as they are. There is a general feeling of acceptance that this process is part and parcel of working life and, much like working life, is totally pointless. Let's face it, this is nothing new, as the Roman army were pretty good at this some 2,000 years ago. The problem is that there are some people who will attempt to put a stop to everything and anything that involves even the tiniest hint of change. Such people are known as Road Blocks. Road Blocks are typically people who love to think that they are the militants raging against the machine when in fact they are intransigent gits and rebels without a cause. The Road Block usually has a limited vocabulary which usually comes out in the following order when faced with the need to change:

- "No."
- "Never."
- "Not on your life."
- "Not over my dead body."
- "I've got an open mind about this, but I think it's a load of bollocks."
- "That's it, we're going on strike."

And all you wanted them to do was move desks. Ask them to do anything more significant and you're up shit creek without a paddle. You see, the Road Block is someone who cannot

see any point in changing; they believe that the working environment is just fine and should be designed around their needs, not their employer's. It also gives them the opportunity to shirk, swing the lead and generally avoid over-exerting themselves. They are the colleagues who will say "This is how I am, so if you can't cope with that, tough"; interpersonal sensitivity is lost on them. When you get a large number of Road Blocks together they are usually called a trade union, and this is where you can have real fun. Unions will strike over many things, some of which are legitimate, such as low pay and poor working conditions. On other occasions, however, they will strike over the most trivial of reasons, such as colleagues being found sleeping on the nightshift, boozing during office hours or distributing crack cocaine to their mates. The Arch Road Block is the union representative who is paid from the subscriptions of his fellow union members to cause disruption and take every opportunity to bring his members out on strike. I heard of one Road Block, working for a government institution, who would attempt to increase union membership by press-ganging non-members into joining. His techniques would range from sweet-talking the new joiners to threatening the longer-standing non-members by calling them scabs. But as one person pointed out to him, they could only be scabs if they were part of the union and refused to go out on strike. To prove how unsuccessful he was, you only needed to see what happened when a strike was called. He would be one of a small handful of people demonstrating outside the establishment. Most people took the day off or drove past offering him the cabman's farewell. Apart from the usual suspects, there are a few other types of Road Block, including:

- **The Crusty.** These are the old farts who are so ancient that they can't do much more than dribble. They are close friends of the Dinosaurs.
- **The Thruster**, the young, up-and-coming Arch Road Block. They see themselves as latter-day leaders of the Luddites who will lead the oppressed in the struggle against their evil employers.
- **The Red Baron.** These people hold deeply socialist viewpoints and want everything to be part of an ideological battle between the proletariat and the bourgeoisie. Hasn't anyone told them that communism collapsed more than ten years ago?

ANNOYANCE RATING

6 – How annoying the Road Block is depends almost entirely on where you sit within the organisation. If you are charged with getting things done then you are likely to find the Road Block's attitude and behaviour somewhat annoying as you will undoubtedly spend hours in tortuous industrial relations meetings debating trivial issues such as car parking spaces for union members. If you happen to be at the bottom of the food chain then you may think them a bit of a hero and may well aspire to becoming like them yourself. In the main, though, the Road Block is a right royal pain in the A.

RARITY

6 – We are told by the management gurus that the frequency of change in organisations is increasing and that we will have to become comfortable with adjusting our behaviours, working practices and skills. But we reach an age where we can't be bothered any more. Once we hit 40 all we want is an easy life, slippers and a cup of cocoa. The thought of keeping up with technology, updating our skills and pretending that we want to change the world is toe curling. So I believe that the numbers of Road Blocks is likely to increase dramatically as the average age of the working population increases.

SEASONAL VARIATIONS

We need to **take a long view** on this one. It's not a simple case of looking at how the Road Block's behaviours change with the passing of the seasons. This is an age- and time-driven thing, which requires us to assess the changes on an annual basis. So watch out for the increasing number of grey-haired and bald-headed men and women in the office, as this should be a leading indicator.

AVOIDANCE|REVENGE STRATEGIES

1. Be flexible and accommodating at work.

2. Get hold of some traffic cones, a few keep out signs and perhaps even some razor wire, and place these around the Road Block's desk.

3. Sack them… it's cheaper in the long run.

4. Say to them "If you're not part of the solution, you're part of the problem."

5. Pose as a union representative and invent some ridiculous reason to go on strike. Bring everyone out and start marching up and down in front of the office with placards, loudhailers and menacing thugs at your side.

☐ Tick here when you have spotted the Road Block

RATE THE
ROAD BLOCK'S
ANNOYANCE

The Sarky Bastard

GENERAL CHARACTERISTICS

They say that sarcasm is the lowest form of wit. Well, in that case, there must be plenty of witty people in the office. Sarcasm is easy. It requires little by way of intelligence or, indeed, skill. What it does require, however, is an acerbic sense of humour coupled with excellent timing and an eye for your colleagues' weak spots. Say hello to the Sarky Bastard. The Sarky Bastard is someone who is expert at the put down and the sharp comment delivered with contempt. They probably need their skulls crushed. However, it's nice to know that the victims of the Sarky Bastard have the Pope on their side. Apparently he has gone on record to say that suffering from the attentions of the Sarky Bastard is the modern form of martyrdom. So the next time you're the butt of some Sarky Bastard's comments, why not write to the Pope and ask his advice? You may well end up as a saint. There are a number types of Sarky Bastard to watch out for, including:

* **The Popper**, who will take every opportunity to take a pop at you.
* **The Setup Merchant** who will set traps for you in order to see you trip up and look like a complete fool.
* **The Comedian**, who makes funny quips about you and your colleagues. They reckon they are just soooo funny.
* **The Offender,** who doesn't know when sarcasm ends and offensive behaviour starts. These are the people who just don't know when to stop and can always be guaranteed to overstep the mark.

The Sarky Bastards will apply their skill in a variety of situations, all of which are designed to belittle their victims. Such situations include:

- Meetings where they will continually have a pop at the other attendees, making funny quips and put downs. I heard of one guy working at an energy company who would sit in meetings and destroy one of his colleagues with immensely contemptuous statements like "Of course the project was going to fail, you were running it," and then follow these up with equally sarcastic comments such as "Naturally, I am only giving you constructive feedback." All this was done in front of the board of directors.
- Social events, when they will make sarcastic comments about your partner: "Blimey, is that your wife? I didn't know you were allowed to bring pets."
- Around the office, when they will make some sarky comment about what you're doing: "Oh, Peter, I didn't know that you came into the office to work."

What's so annoying about Sarky Bastards is that they actually think they are funny and witty when in fact they are neither, nor do they never quite know when to stop. One Sarky Bastard was travelling home with a colleague and was regaling them with a story about their wife who sang in a choral society. The evening before she had been rehearsing in a mental institution and was surrounded by the inmates moaning, dribbling and generally making a nuisance of themselves. The guy was laughing about the situation, when his colleague said "My father is in there," to which the Sarky Bastard replied, "So what's he, the chief executive?" A classic example of a Setup Merchant involved a poor guy who was left a message to ring someone. When he rang them up he was confronted by a barrage of abuse. No matter how hard he tried to calm the annoyed women on the end of the phone, he failed. Everyone around him could see that he was getting incredibly worked up until in the end he slammed the phone down and walked out, not returning until the following morning, still shaken. Only then did the Setup Merchant tell him that it was one of those prank telephone numbers you can ring up. Everyone laughed, except the victim. Setup Merchants are destined to sad, humdrum lives of routine and menial tasks and watching people advance around them. They do add some amusement to a company, though, but don't notice that the last laugh is on them.

ANNOYANCE RATING

3 – To be honest, I quite like Sarky Bastards, so long as they can take as good as they give. The problem, of course, is that many of them don't like the piss being taken out of them, even though they love taking it out of other people. This is their biggest weakness which should be exploited mercilessly. After all, and according to psychological theory, Sarky Bastards only put you down because they are inadequate (small genitals, lowly job, pig ugly, short and deeply insecure – see the Little Big Man), which means they are ideal candidates to practice your revenge strategies on.

RARITY

4 – This varies according to the type and nature of the office in which you work. Some will have a vast number of Sarky Bastards who like to believe their behaviour is part of office banter. They spend most of their working day putting down junior staff, their peers and each other. They love to set each other up, which is funny the first time, but incredibly dull after the fiftieth. In other organisations, and especially those that preach the virtues of political correctness such as government and charitable organisations, there are very few Sarky Bastards indeed.

SEASONAL VARIATIONS

None. There are no seasonal variations in the Sarky Bastard's behaviour. The reason for this is that they have to hide their inadequacies and insecurities by taking the mickey out of everyone around them, all the time.

AVOIDANCE|REVENGE STRATEGIES

1. Just ignore them. As with most morons, it might take some time for it sink in, but in the end they'll have to find some other victim.

2. Build a repertoire of put downs which you can use whenever attacked.

3. Find out the worst thing that ever happened to them and publicise it around the office.

4. Ask your friendly union representative to strike over the excessive use of sarcasm in the office.

5. Punch them in the face. As a violent friend at school once said, "My mother always taught me that actions speak louder than words."

☐ Tick here when you have spotted the Sarky Bastard

RATE THE
SARKY BASTARD'S
ANNOYANCE

The Sinatra

GENERAL CHARACTERISTICS

And now, the end is near, and so I face the final curtain... I'll state my case, of that I'm certain ... and more, much more than this, I did it my way. The enduring tones of Frank Sinatra make any leaving speech a moving event. Well, at least for those lucky enough to be moving on and retiring to an existence which involves more than huddling next to a one-bar heater. Retirement aside, there are those people in the office who, no matter what people expect of them, will always take Frank literally; they will do it their way. Quite frankly (no pun intended) they don't give a monkey's about what people think or what others, including their bosses, want them to do. They will always do everything in the way they want to. They are the Sinatras of the office. They exist at all levels in the organisation and are closely related to some of the other pains you meet, including the Egotist and the Road Block and, unsurprisingly, they are the Control Freak's worst nightmare. The Sinatra is intransigent, dogmatic and stupid. Typical of their attitude, illustrated by one chap's experience, is to call you into their office to gauge your opinion about some terribly important topic only to ignore you and spout on about how they see the problem and how you are going to resolve it. You've guessed it: their way. I mean, what is the point in asking your opinion if they are going to ignore it? Is it an ego thing, are they deaf or do they love winding you up? I heard of one boss who would tell his staff "When I want your opinion, I will give it to you". The same thing happens when any major change is going on in the company. Staff are invited to give their opinions and share their ideas on what is about to happen. The CEO and his team will listen earnestly to the viewpoints expressed with passion, concern and commitment and then dismiss any not aligned with their pre-planned arrangements. Then there are those members of staff who will never heed the

advice and guidance of those people in the office who have more experience; they too insist on doing things their way. One guy who worked in a construction company was a classic Sinatra. He would be given tasks with suitable deadlines, which would require a degree of creative thinking to deliver on time. But he always insisted on completing the task using every step he had learnt at college, taking four times longer than necessary. No matter how often he was counselled on completing his work more rapidly, he insisted on doing it by the book. In the end all he was allowed to do was carry bricks. One of the best stories I heard of came about during a management development course, the sort that involves taking a group of managers away into the mountains to build an effective team. The group concerned had to make their way up to a peak across boggy moorland. Being February, the weather was bitterly cold and wet. Huddling round the map, one of the team suggested they go round the boggy part as they didn't know how deep it was. The team leader had a different idea. He wanted to get to the top as quickly as possible so that he could display his leadership skills. So off he set at a quick pace, marching up towards the boggy area, compelling his team to follow suit. The rest of the team moved off more cautiously. All of a sudden the macho man disappeared from sight. The team continued at their original pace only to find him up to his waist in the freezing cold bog; he looked like a drowned rat, which the team thought highly amusing. So the poor guy had to accept the humiliation of defeat and spent the rest of the day with his wet trousers rubbing against his legs so that by the time they got back to their hostel he was in a bit of a mess. The moral of this story is that Frank Sinatra's music might be good, but you shouldn't take his lyrics literally.

ANNOYANCE RATING

8 – The Sinatra is very annoying. But why? After all, we all love to get our own way and don't like it when we have to cede ground to some over-promoted moron. I can tell you why. It's because they just will not budge; it's their way or the highway.

RARITY

7 – The Sinatra is a pretty common pain. With so many damaged egos and insecure people in the office, we shouldn't be at all surprised that nearly everyone is trying to demonstrate that they are in control and can influence other people to do their bidding. The problem is that this goes against all the advice from our friends in Human Resources who would love all of us to live in happy, team-working coexistence. I'm sorry, but that utopian environment will never exist.

SEASONAL VARIATIONS

The seasonal behaviours of the Sinatra will **vary** according to a number of factors including: how near to retirement they are (there is nothing quite so bad as hearing a retiring CEO stating how this next big project will be their swansong. Of course, when they have gone you can guarantee they'll be blamed for every ill that has befallen the company), appraisal time (when it will have been important to have demonstrated how you have influenced those around you) and, of course, party time, when a collection of Tree-Huggers and Extracurriculars will be jockeying for poll position on the organising committee.

AVOIDANCE|REVENGE STRATEGIES

1. Ignore them and do it your way. If you can't beat them, why not join the increasing ranks of Sinatras in your office?

2. Send them off to a Buddhist monastery where they can learn how to accept other people's opinions.

3. Challenge them to an arm-wrestling match. Whoever wins can decide on what to do and how to do it.

4. Bring a Karaoke machine into the office and play *My Way*.

5. Run them over in the car park.

☐ Tick here when you have spotted the Sinatra

RATE THE
SINATRA'S
ANNOYANCE

The Space Invader

Everyone likes to have space. In the home, at work or when out shopping. As someone who used to get claustrophobic in crowds, I can empathise with anyone who complains of people invading their personal territory. Mind you, when it comes to the office, I'm sure that no one wants their space invaded by anyone, let alone some creep with dandruff, halitosis, psoriasis and yellow teeth. The Space Invader is someone who fails to appreciate that we all need space. Space is important because it signals many things including the beginning and end of a conversation, how friendly we are to others and, of course, how intimate we are with those around us. Indeed according to eminent psychologists, there are four zones of interpersonal space:

- The intimate zone, which extends from 0 to 45 centimetres. So the next time someone comes this close, just pray that your wife or husband aren't around. And, I guess that how close to zero you might find yourself will depend on size and perhaps position. We can also safely assume that if you are at zero centimetres you will probably be naked and in a hotel room, or perhaps draped over a photocopier.
- The personal zone, which starts at 45 centimetres and ends at 120 centimetres. When someone comes this close, you could shout "you getting personal?" and deploy your canister of mace. This zone is clearly a key one for office staff as many insist on filling up their space with personal effects which in the main comprise fluffy gonks with sickly "I love you" messages hanging out of their bottoms, plastic junk retrieved from fast food restaurants' bins and contrived pictures of their loved ones.
- The social zone (or pub) which covers 120 to 360 centimetres. This is where we spend time with our friends (notice not colleagues) chatting, laughing and gossiping about the jerks we work with and for.

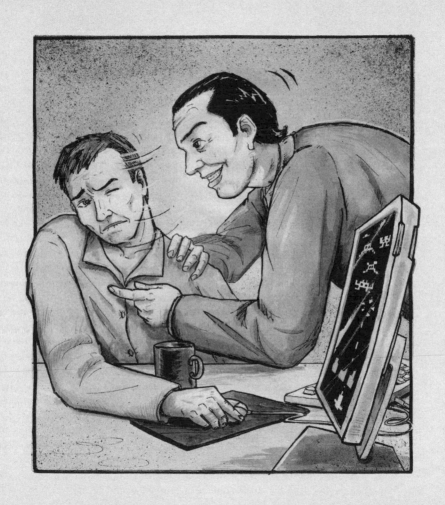

• The public zone which goes from 360 to 750 centimetres and beyond. I reckon the only place you can get this much space is on a mountain. Mind you, I think that most chief executive's palatial offices fall into this zone, which must explain their ability to keep away from their staff (often called "professional distance").

There is a simple rule of thumb – the higher your position the bigger your zone. So pity the poor old call centre operative who is well and truly stuck in cattle-like conditions found in the intimate zone. I do have a problem with the personal zone. The loos in most offices are just too close for comfort. Sitting down and getting on with business with someone next door isn't pleasant (as we have seen with the Bowel Mover), and the same is true for the urinals. Shouldn't they be miles apart? The Space Invader hates wasting any time in the public or social zones. These zones harbour too many feelings of rejection for them, so they aim to spend as much time in the personal and intimate zones as they can. This can be disconcerting. Their tactics include sitting on your desk and making idle conversation whilst you do your best to ignore them, cornering you at the coffee machine and attempting to use some of your desk space for their paraphernalia. A male Space Invader working in an investment bank was feared by all, not because he was a bully but because he was one of those overbearing middle-aged men, recently divorced, who didn't look after his personal hygiene particularly well. He would go up to the people he needed to speak to and, instead of standing a healthy distance away, would push his face to within a couple of inches of his victim. Each time he did this, the victim would lurch backwards and attempt to move away only to be pursued. As he talked (more shouted, really), the person opposite would be sprayed by his spit and suffocated by his halitosis. His favourite tactic was to corner his colleagues by the water cooler where there was no escape. In the end they had a whip round and bought him some personal hygiene products. The reverse of the Space Invader is the Territorialist who has every right to defend their patch against insurgents who are hell bent on taking the space of others. Unlike on the train, such people are less offensive although you do get the odd one or two people who are obsessive about their chairs which cannot be adjusted. They will leave notices warning people of the dire consequences of moving the said chair. This is, of course, a red rag to a bull and the chairs are usually adjusted and moved around the office on a regular basis.

ANNOYANCE RATING

8 – I hate people invading my space and I am sure you do too. There is nothing worse than someone getting too close for comfort. You feel disconcerted, under attack and vulnerable. I believe there should be a European Rule on Space at Work with draconian fines and prison sentences for those that break it.

RARITY

8 – With so many people enduring cramped working conditions, the Space Invader is becoming more and more common. With hot desking, cost cutting and other measures leading to increased pokiness, I fully expect there to be rebellion soon as disgruntled workers run amok and overrun senior executives' palatial offices.

SEASONAL VARIATIONS

You will see more Space Invaders during the **party season** when the false sense of jollity will bring out the Space Invader in us all. At this time of year we all let our barriers down and enjoy a bit of an invasion. Come January and it's back to our trenches.

AVOIDANCE/REVENGE STRATEGIES

1. Place a wire frame around your body which can be used to delineate the boundary of your personal space which must not be crossed.

2. Scent mark your personal territory with urine. This should keep even the most ardent Space Invader at bay.

3. Install tank traps around your desk and watch as the Space Invader's invasion fails horribly.

4. Build a space detector that allows you to determine which zone (intimate, personal, social and public) people are in. Make sure it has suitable noises and colours to make it helpful to your blind and deaf colleagues.

5. Dress up as Captain Kirk and march around the office shouting "Space, the final frontier".

☐ Tick here when you have spotted the Space Invader

RATE THE **SPACE INVADER'S** ANNOYANCE

The Stress Junkie

GENERAL CHARACTERISTICS

Apparently, a bad day at the office can be more unhealthy than domestic strife, unsafe sex or taking drugs. Moreover, a stressful job can lead to addictions, impotence and relationship problems. According to the latest research, stress at work has now reached crisis point with 90 million days lost every year in the UK alone, costing British industry something in the region of £3.7 billion per annum. It seems that even poor old Tony Blair couldn't cope with his demanding life of spin. Suffering a heart scare, the hapless Prime Minister spent a nervous few hours in hospital. He and so many of our colleagues are suffering from what is commonly known as competitive stress disorder, or CSD. It's oh so now to be under intense stress. If you're not, then quite frankly you're not worth a candle. CSD is the urge to complain incessantly about your stress levels whether or not you are stressed at all. In fact most of the moaning minnies out there are merely trying to hide the fact that they do no work at all or are such bad time managers that they can't deliver anything on time. How many times have I heard phrases like "I'm maxed out," "I haven't got time to think," "I can't seem to get my work/life balance right when I'm working fifteen-hour days, looking after my disabled mother, bringing up my thirty foster children, working out three hours a day at the gym and helping out at the local hospice"? Blimey, even civil servants complain about being stressed these days, so things must have got bad. Let's face it, people in the government's employ barely raise a sweat in the seven hours they work every day (or is it week?), but it's a great way to get time off work. And when the union gets involved the possibility of taking a six-month break from the daily grind is a distinct possibility. The press love it too, publishing articles about individuals who just can't cope with the trials and tribulations of their work (which they chose to pursue, remember).

Everyone complains, from city workers to professional singers. According to other research, cleaners, food preparers, carpenters and lab technicians fall within the top twenty of the stressful jobs chart. I guess I can see why cleaning up other people's excrement might be stressful (especially if you have no gloves) but sawing wood? Celebrities too love to complain about how tough their lives are; yeah, I guess it must be really tough being obsessed with the public eye and taking every opportunity to boost your enormous ego. And it's not just celebs. I heard of a builder who was having problems starting his chainsaw. Having tried to start it a dozen times, he flipped, walked to the rear of his van, picked up his sledgehammer and laid into the offending equipment until it lay in pieces before him. I was also told of a salesman who was having a particularly heated debate with a customer on his mobile phone. At the end of the conversation he opened the window and threw the phone onto the busy street, some ten storeys below.

ANNOYANCE RATING

7 – Stress Junkies are annoying because they like to create the impression that they are not only busy but also indispensable. It's not enough to be stressed, but they feel they have to outdo their fellow sufferers of CSD. If someone quips that they have worked sixty hours, the Stress Junkie will say they worked a hundred. The stress stakes are high and the Stress Junkie plays to win.

RARITY

9 – In these technology-intensive days the Stress Junkie is king. Modern communication such as mobile phones, wireless email systems and laptops all help to feed stress-addicted employees. It gives them every excuse to complain about how busy, stressed and important they are. Technology never sleeps, so nor should they. This is definitely a pain on the increase. Only when we revert to a pastoral existence will we see a reduction. But then the Stress Junkie will complain that they are bored tugging at cow's tits all day. Fortunately, the effects of adrenalin and cortisol will ensure they have their first heart attack before they are forty. Hopefully then they'll shut up, perhaps permanently.

SEASONAL VARIATIONS

A Stress Junkie's behaviour normally peaks around any deadline, no matter how trivial. So you should expect to see them **all day, every day**.

AVOIDANCE|REVENGE STRATEGIES

1. Offer the Stress Junkie a CD of whale song to calm their nerves.

2. Suggest to them that if they can't stand the heat, they should get out of the kitchen. Quite frankly, if they can't cut it they should get a job as a milkman or a paperboy and quit complaining.

3. Paint your eyes with some particularly thick eyeliner or mascara and attempt to outdo your fellow Stress Junkies by looking like the living dead. When asked, just say you haven't slept for three days because you have been soooo busy.

4. Recommend that they go on a bread making course which will help them to focus their stress and aggression, and maybe they could make something tasty which they could share with their colleagues.

5. Give them a pile more work to do and tell them that you want it by eight o'clock the next morning.

☐ Tick here when you have spotted the Stress Junkie

RATE THE
STRESS JUNKIE'S
ANNOYANCE

The Teflon and Marigold

GENERAL CHARACTERISTICS

As a scout, washing up pans caked in grease and burnt on food was a real drag. What made the whole experience ten times worse was the mess it made of my hands; fingernails embedded with pieces of fat and bacon and skin shrivelled from the filthy water. Later on in life I discovered the value of Marigold rubber gloves and Teflon-coated frying pans. Not only could you protect your hands from the corrosive effects of contaminated water, but you could also remove even the most stubborn of food remnants from the saucepan without destroying it in the process. Ah the joy of Teflon and Marigold. A few years beyond my discovery of the slippery benefits of these two technologies, I found that they were heavily utilised within the office environment, with the same slippery characteristics. Whilst working on a major project I used to hear colleagues refer to a couple of managers as Teflon and Marigold. I wondered why on earth they were called that. After all, when someone is a useless idiot, they are usually given much worse names than that, like "arsehole" for instance. When I enquired why they were given such nicknames, I was merely told "nothing sticks". Then I understood what they meant. The Teflon and Marigold seems to get away with murder. No matter how bad their behaviour, how incredibly incompetent they are, or how enormous their cock-ups, they somehow get away scot-free without any comeback whatsoever. As my colleagues quite rightly observed, nothing sticks. Not only is this annoying for those of us who receive regular drubbings from our evil bosses, but it also feels as though justice is never done. If the budding Teflon and Marigold is looking for a role model, they need look no further than Tony Blair. At present Tony is king of the Teflons. That's the art of the Teflon and Marigold, they always get away with it. How they survive is a bit of a mystery, especially when so many others fall along the wayside. They rarely have the skill of the Butt Licker, the aptitude of the Politician, or

the finesse of the Competitor. I believe that in many cases they are just too stupid to realise what's going on around them which suggests that Darwin's theory has broken down. Then again, there are those species that have survived which shouldn't have, so perhaps the Teflon and Marigold is one of life's great survivors. I guess there must be a few Teflon and Marigolds who are actually experts at avoiding blame and are using their higher order delegation, deflection, and deception skills to ensure someone else carries the can. There was one man who was expert at avoiding the blame for anything that went wrong, even when it was his fault. He would direct a project and other such initiatives with the panache of a drowned rat, and yet when these initiatives failed his subordinates would be sacked. But when they succeeded he took the glory to the exclusion of his staff (classic Leech behaviour). In the end, those that still worked with him decided to get their own back. The trap involved creating a bogus deal with a fictitious client. As the deal was so large, the Teflon and Marigold spent a lot of time telling the CEO how great he was and what a killer deal it was going to be. The company invested many tens of thousands on securing the deal only to find that the whole thing was a total con. And because the Teflon and Marigold had not bothered to check out the deal, he was at last found out. This time it did stick.

ANNOYANCE RATING

8 – We hate them for the simple reason that they seem to slip past all the nets and traps set out to either stitch them up or to establish accountability. The Teflon and Marigold is always clean, perhaps too squeaky clean, in the eyes of the boss, despite the fact that everyone else knows just how rubbish they are.

RARITY

3 – In these days, where accountability is king, the Teflon and Marigold finds it increasingly difficult to escape the retribution and persecution they deserve. At last we are finally seeing CEOs falling on their swords for the misdemeanours of their staff – or their own, of course. For years they have escaped, allowing their staff to take the rap for their sins. But as Warren Buffett once said, "When the tide goes out, you can see who is swimming naked." Of course, those Teflon and Marigolds who are high enough up in the organisation will walk away with a big bag of cash which they can stash for when they get out of jail.

SEASONAL VARIATIONS

The principal variation in the Teflon and Marigold's behaviour tends to exhibit itself near **appraisal time**. During this sensitive period they will ensure anything that has gone badly during the year does not have their name associated with it. And of course, they will make sure that all the successes have their name firmly attached.

AVOIDANCE|REVENGE STRATEGIES

1. Avoid anyone with sloping shoulders, a sure sign of a Teflon and Marigold.

2. Hold a blamestorming session to ensure they carry the can. This session involves sitting in a group to discuss why something went wrong. Of course what really happens is that it will become a shouting match and potentially a fist fight. So long as the Teflon and Marigold gets it, who cares?

3. Leave some greasy pots and pans on their desk together with some rubber gloves and ask them to clean them up.

4. Put them in touch with an agency who specialise in placing people in cleaning jobs.

5. Create a wanted poster, complete with a suitable reward and picture of the Teflon and Marigold. Have a headline such as "Wanted for Escaping Accountability" and post them around the office.

☐ Tick here when you have spotted the Teflon and Marigold

RATE THE
TEFLON AND MARIGOLD'S
ANNOYANCE

The Tree-Hugger

There are some incredibly happy people at work. They exude friendliness, joy, wackiness and fun. Thank god there aren't too many of them. The Tree-Hugger is the preserve of the HR Department and those irrepressible figures who appear so happy all the time that you have to question what they are on. Whatever it is, can we have some too? Tree-Huggers are characterised by their use of superlatives; you know, words like brilliant, fabulous, super and wonderful. One contributor told me of a chap in their office who would say "fantastic" all the time. She managed to count 37 in one day alone and on most days he uttered that magic word on at least 20 occasions. The Tree-Hugger's destiny is to create a level playing field in which everyone loves each other, finds some intrinsic happiness in turning up for work every day and is honoured to be treated with contempt and get paid rubbish. It reminds me of fast food restaurants which create a false image of fun by making their staff wear garish uniforms with badges proclaiming them to be a member of the crew or employee of the month. If staff buy into this, then they are more stupid than I thought. Tree-Huggers come in a variety of guises, including:

- **The Treacly Trainer,** who insists on delivering training events in a caring, sharing and politically correct way, which normally involves patronising the audience and treating them like morons.
- **The Cosy Coach**, who will apply all of their skills to uncover your innermost thoughts and desires and then nod in a sincere way to make out that they understand what the hell you're talking about. Remember, these people are only doing this because they are nosey (see the Nosey Parker).

- **The Ice-Breaking Idiot**, who at key events or at the start of a brainstorming or training session will invent crackpot ways of getting everyone to know each other. This typically involves members of staff doing something stupid like telling the others what animal, flower or car they would like to be. Such Ice-Breakers are received with the contempt they deserve and are normally known as the creeping death.

Things don't always go to plan for the Tree-Hugger. On one occasion a number of senior executives were whisked off to a retreat where they were to spend three days discussing the organisation's strategy. At the opening session all were asked to reveal something about themselves that nobody else knew. It was all going fine until one middle-aged lady confessed to being a lesbian. It was not really the time or place for that sort of revelation and the poor old men who were with her went very red and clammed up for the rest of the retreat. Another, and perhaps even worse event, involved the Tree-Hugger taking an entire executive team of a company away to a ski resort in order to build them into a high-performing top team. The idea was that they would spend time getting to know each other, discussing strategy and skiing. Within a few hours they were at each others' throats and rather than forming a team, broke off into small groups vowing to spend their time apart and never speak to each other again. So much for teamwork. The Tree-Hugger is someone who is heavily into the latest HR fad which is sweeping the corporate world. The current one is all about the need to get in touch with our emotional and spiritual sides and involves pretending to be Inuit or medieval farmers. I'm sorry, but such stuff is utter shite. What's more, so is the latest view from HR that we all need regular emotional audits to help us deal with the toxic emotions in the workplace. Apparently the insensitive or incompetent behaviour of our colleagues and bosses can cause ordinary negative emotions to become toxic. And? But there is perhaps an even more worrying trend – down-aging. It seems that Generation X has been hit by a wave of immaturity and that anyone between the ages of 18 and 49 is now considered to be a rejuvenile. So now you have every excuse to act like a child at the office.

ANNOYANCE RATING

6 –Tree-Huggers are too happy for their own good. Their sickening sense of joy and flaky, fluffy, content-free nature is enough to turn anyone to drink. Most people in the office are relatively even-keeled when it comes to emotions; they are sad most of the time, happy some of the time and ecstatic at 5.00 p.m. Few feel bouncy every second of every day. And those that do are just too over the top and nauseating for their own good.

RARITY

3 – Compared to the headcount of a typical company, the number of Tree-Huggers is relatively few. Mind you, if there are too many you might as well work in a holiday camp. This provides an environment where you can be wacky all of the time and never grow up.

SEASONAL VARIATIONS

Christmas and any other annual events in the company calendar will bring out a veritable forest of Tree-Huggers, all desperate to make the celebrations fun. They would have everyone in the office dressed up as Santa Claus and his elves and force them all to enjoy themselves.

AVOIDANCE|REVENGE STRATEGIES

1. Bring a chainsaw to work and cut down the trees. Soon there won't be any left for the Tree-Huggers to hug.

2. Take a baseball bat to their head.

3. Make them do some real work and see how they cope.

4. Sabotage one of their events by arranging some alternative entertainment such as naked mud wrestling and watch them get a severe drubbing.

5. Set up a national miserable day in which anyone who smiles must pay £1,000 to charity.

☐ Tick here when you have spotted the Tree-Hugger

RATE THE
TREE-HUGGER'S
ANNOYANCE

The Village Idiot

GENERAL CHARACTERISTICS

Despite the mantra of education, education, education, we are woefully short of competent people. Perhaps if more people studied something vocational the workplace might not be full of idiots. Unfortunately most students love to study subjects such as Advanced Tap Dancing rather than something that might be considered useful. So no matter where you work you will bump into one, two, or perhaps thirty cranially challenged individuals. Such people are known as Village Idiots. In medieval times the most stupid person in the village would be singled out for special treatment; they would be ridiculed, laughed at and pestered most of the time. Every village had one and indeed would be somewhat lost without them. The reason why we often hear about Village Idiots is because they provide such amusement. Here are a few stories:

- The lawyer who, when attempting to demonstrate how safe the windows were to a bunch of law students, fell to his death 24 floors below when the window shattered.
- The gas company employees who, on investigating a major leak at a factory, decided to use a lighter to guide their way though the darkened building. Apparently neither of them were seen again and the wreckage was spread over a number of miles.
- The office worker who was seen forcing her credit card into the floppy drive of her computer. When asked what she was doing she responded "shopping on the Internet".
- The secretary who, on running out of paper, asked her colleague what she ought to do. When told to use the photocopier paper, the secretary went over to the photocopier, popped her last unused piece in and made five blank copies.

- The investment banker who accidentally copied the entire global bank's staff into an email. By the time it had reached H in the address book, all the mail servers had crashed around the world. He was, as you might expect in such a tolerant organisation, sacked.
- The IT support guy who would email passwords to new employees to allow them to activate their email accounts.
- The executive who complained that his computer screen had gone blank and that he needed a new one. The technical support chap came up, moved the mouse and the screen came back on. The executive hadn't realised that his screen saver was on.

According to some well publicised research, Village Idiots suffer from the double whammy of following the wrong course of action whilst simultaneously believing they are doing just fine. Stupid people actually believe they are competent and are blissfully unaware of how dangerously dim-witted they are. In my mind, Darwin was right when he said "Ignorance more frequently begets confidence than does knowledge." Apparently it's all down to their metacognitive skills, but for god's sake don't try and explain that to them. The Village Idiot is another case where Darwin's theory breaks down. Technically such people should have been eliminated from the gene pool long ago, but it is clear from the number of intellectual lightweights we come across in our working lives that stupid people can survive. You can normally spot a Village Idiot a mile off. They often have a pained look on their face, as though it's all they can do keep themselves alive, let alone think. Their jaw will be slack, their brow furrowed and they will have that vacant, "no one's at home" look about them.

ANNOYANCE RATING

6 – Having to explain to a moron what to do is nothing short of futile. By the time you have explained how he or she needs to file a letter you might as well have done it yourself. The Village Idiot is intensely annoying because you just can't get through. They smile inanely signalling to you that they are alive, but not much else. You can stare into their blank eyes with little hope of a response. I guess the worst bit is the smile.

RARITY

5 – According to recent surveys there are 11 million incompetent people in the workplace in the UK alone. Despite the drive to raise the educational standards of the young, I don't hold out much hope for a dramatic fall in the quantity of Village Idiots. But with the increased use of technology (which replaces the work of cretins) and an increasing preponderance to push work overseas, their numbers should drop sharply. But wait a minute. The only problem with this is that you'll then start to find more of them working in fast food joints and other low wage outlets where brain cells are already in short supply.

SEASONAL VARIATIONS

None. The Village Idiot is far too simple to recognise any change in the seasons, so we shouldn't expect any variations in their amoeba-like behaviour either.

AVOIDANCE|REVENGE STRATEGIES

1. Screen anyone you work with (or for) for Village Idiot tendencies. If they show them, try to avoid working with them.

2. Set up some stocks in the office, secure the Village Idiot in them, and invite your colleagues to throw rotten vegetables.

3. Knock them on the head repeatedly and shout "Hello! Hello! Is anybody in there?"

4. Suggest they surf the website for the Darwin Awards, which honour those who improve our gene pool by removing themselves from it.

5. Ask them to spot the difference between an amoeba and their brain. If they look confused work with the amoeba.

☐ Tick here when you have spotted the Village Idiot

RATE THE
VILLAGE IDIOT'S
ANNOYANCE

Afterword

§ o you have been abused by them, frustrated by them, and had your work disrupted by them. Everywhere you look around the office you see Pains. You may have also realised that you too are a Pain and by now have recognised which category (or categories) you fall into. So how do you avoid being a Pain yourself? Here are my top five ways:

1. Pain Spot (obviously).
2. Keep your head down, be industrious and don't get in anyone's way.
3. Get a job that keeps you out of the office.
4. Rise to Chief Executive so you have a room on your own and won't be disturbed.
5. Retire.

And finally, please remember the Five Golden Rules for Pain Spotting. They will help you live a fulfilled, happy and enriched life.

1. NEVER JUDGE A BOOK BY ITS COVER
You mustn't be fooled by initial appearances. What at first glance may seem like a commonplace Bully might actually turn out to be a Tree-Hugger who has lost the plot. Likewise, a straightforward Nosey Parker may in fact be a fully-fledged Gossip. First impressions count, sure, but exchanging views with a Bowel Mover might be somewhat career-limiting.

2. DON'T BE COMPLACENT IN YOUR PAIN SPOTTING

Pains, like all other species on the planet and according to Darwin, are able to adapt, evolve, mutate and cross-fertilize, occasionally leaving you with a chameleon-like being to contend with. In this way, a Midas may also be a Corrupt Bastard, a Ball-Breaker a part-time Career Bike. There's nothing to stop you ticking off more than one Pain per observation. So, make your observations; do your analysis, and be sure you have got all the qualities of every Pain straight before committing yourself.

3. REMEMBER, THERE'S NO SUCH THING AS THE MORAL HIGH GROUND HERE

The reasons for this are two-fold. First off, this book is about providing an amusing diversion during your working life. Second, we are all Pains of one form or another, and as the saying goes, "People in glass houses shouldn't drop their guts in an office toilet".

4. DON'T GET INTO ANY FIST FIGHTS

Any suggestions that "the book told me to do it" are like a tower of jelly – they won't stand up in a court of law.

5. LEARN TO LOVE YOUR PAIN

This is the trickiest and most testing of all the Golden Rules. But you should learn to love the Pain. For he is your brother. Or your Diet Bore colleague. The Bible tells us to love our neighbours. And that means unconditionally. Even when the person next to you is eating the most disgusting concoction around. Besides, if you don't learn to love them, you might just go mad.